Mavericks
on
Tap

Creating Organisations that Deliver Awesome Outcomes

Peter Johns

PBJ Publishing, P.O. Box 5015
Laburnum, Victoria 3130, Australia.

www.pbj.com.au

First Edition 2015

National Library of Australia Cataloguing-in-Publication entry

Johns, Peter, author.

Mavericks on Tap : creating organisations that deliver awesome outcomes / Peter Johns

ISBN: 978-0-646-93688-8 (paperback)

Subjects: Organisational behaviour, Organisational change, Corporate culture, Employees--Attitudes

Dewey Number: 302.35

Copyright © 2015 Peter Johns

Dedication

**In memory of my father -
a true Maverick who never
stopped challenging the status quo**

Acknowledgments

There have been many people who have made this book possible, and to whom I owe a debt of thanks. Janine Johnston and Debbie Hilton who challenged me to write it in the first place, and the extraordinary effort, especially from Janine, in reading and rereading drafts.

To all those who read drafts and gave valuable insights and comments, especially: Greg Altamore, Adrienne de Kretser Julianne and Andy Hearn, Ian Jasper, Peter Johnston, Geoff Mabbett, Nigel Pugh and Lisa Speakman.

Special thanks to Matt Johnston for the marvellous illustrations and cover. This is his first publication as well!

To all those people who have helped me over the years to gain some insight into how organisations work.

And finally to my wife Diane, who not only provided valuable commentary during the writing of this book, but lived through most of the experiences as well – even if it was just (or most importantly!) the debriefing after a hard day at the office!

Contents

1 Introduction

"There is no such thing as a new idea. It is impossible. We simply take a lot of old ideas and put them into a sort of mental kaleidoscope. We give them a turn and they make new and curious combinations. We keep on turning and making new combinations indefinitely; but they are the same old pieces of colored glass that have been in use through all the ages." – Mark Twain

Mavericks are those people who challenge the status quo. They want to make a difference to the value achieved from desired outcomes and the ways things are done. The longevity of successful organisations, whether a commercial enterprise, government authority, sporting club, community group, religious institution – anywhere that people seek to work together for a common cause, is dependent on the successful integration of the Maverick.

Some organisations struggle to fully understand the value of the Maverick. Other organisations find it difficult to contain the Mavericks over-enthusiastic zeal. While organisations strive for innovation and improved performance, they often subdue and repress those who challenge the imbedded practices and processes that hinder change. This they do at their own peril.

How often do we hear managers' spruik the innovation mantra? "We need to be more innovative in the way we work". Some organisations create "innovation teams". They even create services contracts that have "innovation committees" with key performance indicators that try to measure and reward innovation. Some even declare "innovation" as a core value, with performance plans and position descriptions littered with the word.

Innovation is often seen as the Holy Grail, an end in itself. This is where the shortcomings arise – like the quest for the Holy Grail. The crusaders of the Middle Ages searched for a holy relic in which they believed lay power and redemption, yet those things had already been passed on millennia before. The quest for the grail gave them a purpose, but it didn't really achieve outcomes of significant value.

We need to go beyond innovation. It is not innovation that we are really striving for; it is the creation of awesome outcomes. I was once asked by a senior manager why I worked in the water industry. My reply was simple – to make a positive difference. Any change, no matter how large or small, that improves the performance of an organisation and the lives of those it influences is an awesome outcome. Mark Twain penned it well above. Awesome outcomes do not happen as a light globe, eureka moment. An awesome outcomes is more often than not the result of taking an idea from someone else and applying it to the situation at hand and doing things differently.

To allow such things to happen often requires a paradigm shift in our organisational culture – mostly because we are creatures of habit and change creates anxiety. Anxiety generates resistance and a reluctance to embrace different ways of working together. I remember my father assisting me with the office management when I started up my consulting business. He had been a primary school principal and had exceptional organisational skills. However, managing the accounts and invoicing required using a computer, which was not one of his strongest skillsets. The secretary came up to me one day and said, "Your father is getting upset with me because you keep changing the finance system just when he gets used to it". I thought I was just making it more efficient! What I was actually doing was creating frustration and anxiety, which was transferred onto the poor secretary.

Throughout my working life I have had the opportunity to experiment with changing and challenging the way things have been done in a number of organisations. I have been able to test the theories of others and have also been able to develop a few my own. While this has mostly been within the water industry, the principles have translated well into other organisations.

Being innovative and looking at alternative ways to achieve outcomes can lead to awesome results. However, it can also be very costly, both in financial and human capital. Managing the risks associated with the implementation of new ideas is critically important. There is also the "dark" side of organisational behaviour that can hinder any attempt to improve performance. This is why we need to think beyond innovation and carefully reflect on how our organisations are structured and deal with the shadows that lurk within.

The first part of the book looks at the nature of working together, the role and essence of the Maverick, and the integration of the Maverick within an organisation. The middle part discusses some theory around organisational boundaries, a model for the incorporation Mavericks within organisations, and managing transitions. The last part of the book examines the darker side of organisations, managing risks and the concept of organisational reflection.

This book is not a step by step instructions guide for creating awesome outcomes or the definitive works on how to manage Mavericks. It is a collection of ideas and experiences brought together to provide a framework and an approach to organisational structure for developing awesome outcomes, with plenty of real life illustrations!

Enjoy!

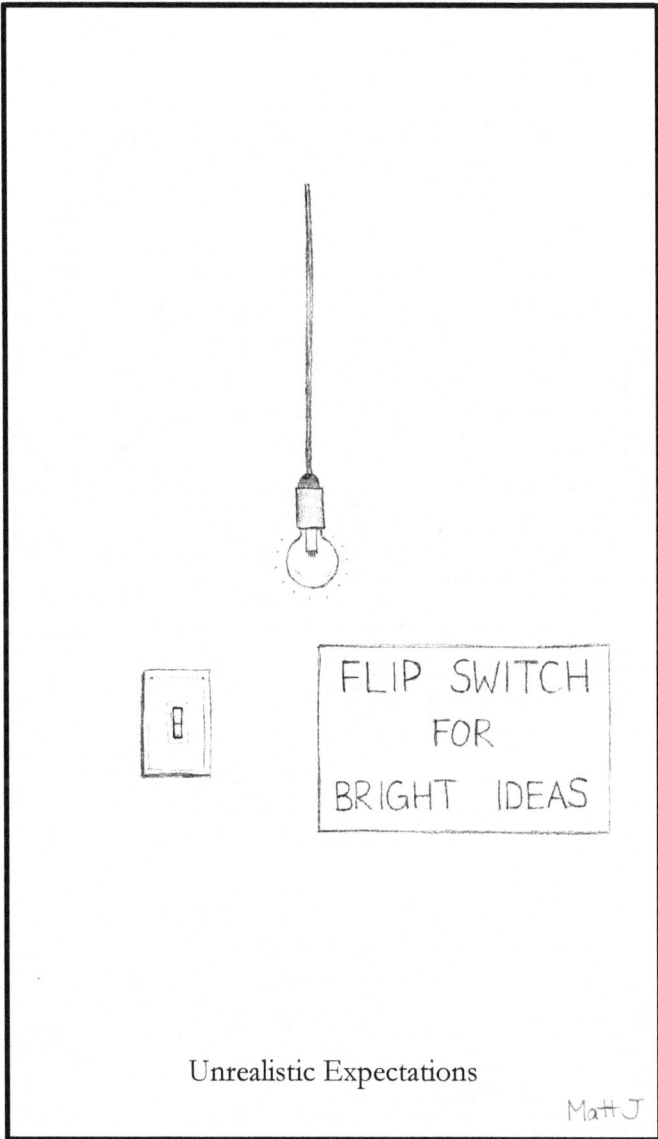

FLIP SWITCH
FOR
BRIGHT IDEAS

Unrealistic Expectations

Matt J

2   Sharing Stories

"The purpose of a storyteller is not to tell you how to think, but to give you questions to think upon." - Brandon Sanderson

Soon after we were married, my wife and I travelled to India for three months to study aid and development. We were both interested in seeing what sort of difference we could make by working in a developing country. She was working for an international aid organisation in their marketing section and I was working for a large engineering consulting firm involved in water-related projects.

The study program was run by a small Indian aid organisation. We usually spent the morning studying aid and development theory. There was an incredible group of lecturers from India, Australia and the United States. It was wonderful to have a strong Indian viewpoint, which was a paradigm shift from the usual western paternalistic perspective we were so often used to hearing. As part of the program we also spent some time each day working in an urban slum in New Delhi called Nehru Place.

The slum was really an itinerant work camp for the labourers who were building the surrounding multi-storey buildings. Most of the inhabitants had been poor subsistence farmers who had moved to the city to find work to feed and support their families. This is a situation that is familiar to many large cities as they grow.

The slum consisted of dilapidated shanties constructed from scavenged materials and homemade bricks. Narrow laneways furrowed their way through the shanties, with open drains always carrying murky water whether it was raining or not. Our first impression was that it smelled awful, but it didn't take long for our senses to adjust.

The people in the slum were very friendly. My wife assisted with a crèche while I worked with a group of labourers on building projects. Our language skills were very poor, but we managed to get by. The people were also very gracious and were often sharing a cup of "chai" with us (a very sweet milky Indian tea). Those with the least are often the most generous.

One of the lessons we learned early was about sharing.

We were living in shared accommodation with about ten other people. We had an Indian cook who provided us with hot spicy food, which took us a while to get accustomed to (both the spicy food and having our food cooked for us). Sometimes we would go into the slum for a whole day. We took our own lunch, mostly cut sandwiches prepared by our cook. He always over-catered. When we had finished our lunch on our first full day visit to the slum we had plenty of food left over. We asked the project leader whether it would be a good idea to give the leftover food to some of the people in the slum. It would be a shame for it to go to waste. His response was not what we expected.

He said that if we had invited some of the people to come and share our lunch with them that would have been very generous indeed. They had, after all, often invited us into their homes to share a cup of chai. However, if we distributed only the remains of our lunch, it could be interpreted that only our leftovers and scraps were good enough to share with the people in the slum. Here we were thinking how good we were giving our time "helping" people, when showing a little bit of dignity and respect by inviting them to share our lunch would have been so much more valuable. So humbling.

Many years later I was working for a metropolitan water authority as the planning manager at one of its very large sewage treatment plants (servicing more than two million people). One afternoon I was making my way to a managers' meeting and noticed that the operators were feasting on a nice little buffet of food in the control room. When I sat down with the other managers I made some witty remark about the operations budget needing to be trimmed if they could afford such lavish lunches. I was bluntly informed by the operations manager that the executive team had held their monthly meeting at the plant earlier in the day and the food was the leftovers. So I imparted my experience about sharing food from the slums in India.

It is sometimes surprising how a well-placed story can affect the status quo of an organisation. The water authority had been seeking to move to a flatter, more equitable structure, with core values of respect and integrity. Yet this small example illustrated the disparity in the benefits that senior managers enjoyed. It was a small thing, but from that time on people tended to take more care regarding how others were treated in the organisation. A month later my manager arranged a lunch for the managers and invited the operations and maintenance staff to attend as well!

◆ ◆ ◆

The ability to create awesome outcomes is greatly enhanced when there is an openness to share stories and our life experiences. While they may not directly be related to the task at hand, they can provide the catalyst for rethinking how we go about our everyday activities.

Sometimes stories take on a life of their own and enter into the urban folklore. I had worked on upgrading one of the largest sporting stadiums in our city, an international icon, and I had a set of the drawings squirrelled away in my garage. I was looking for a way to visualise how much water was treated every day at the sewage treatment plant. I calculated the volume of water that could be held by the stadium if it were filled to the top and determined the number of times it would need to be filled every day. I had used the number in a few presentations around the water authority. Decades later, I still hear people quoting the number times the stadium fills when describing the treatment plant. It makes me chuckle at how widely the number varies.

Stories create a non-threatening way of sharing ideas. They allow people to reflect about concepts and consequences and how they relate to daily living. When they are woven around basic common-sense principles they can be very effective communication tools. These stories can have significant longevity. One need go no further than the parables of the Jesus or the fables of Aesop. I do not believe that it matters what the source or the authenticity of the story is; only that it represents a good idea.

I have structured this book around telling stories. Many of the stories are recollections from personal experience, some are events I have observed, and some I have read or heard about. They all seem pertinent to the ideas that are being expressed. In as much as the stories presented are my view of the world, I am sure that there are some who would challenge the accuracy of some of my recollections. I make no apologies for this; a good story is always a good story, regardless of the facts, and as such, I have deliberately not made mention of specific names or places.

Here are a few suggestions for creating a positive environment for telling stories:

- All people have stories to tell. It is important to provide some space for the more quiet and timid to share their experiences.
- I have often provided time in team meetings for someone to share an experience. I am also very careful to limit the time people get to do this.
- When sharing stories, watch for the interpersonal cues that the audience is losing interest (e.g. looking at their watch, shuffling their feet.)
- Keep a diary of interesting events. It can be valuable to read over, years later, with a little more wisdom and experience.
- Listening to stories is often more important than telling stories.

Awesome Outcome Principle:

Creating an environment where people can exchange life experiences can provide a catalyst for cultural change and awesome outcomes.

Not a good choice for the "wolf" Prince!!"

Post Script

I have shared this food story with people in many organisations over the years and it has often had a positive effect on their working environment. The inability to treat others with dignity and respect is reflected in the practices and processes within the places we work. This is most noticeable when benefits not related to work or output are given to the selected few.

A memorable example involved the introduction of total remuneration packages at the water authority. As a concept, total remuneration packages were supposed to include the value of all the fringe benefits received by an employee, such as motor vehicles, so that the salaries were seen as equitable across the organisation. However, in this case, the executive put restrictions on the access to a vehicle and the type of vehicle an employee could receive.

Staff below line managers were not allowed to have a car in their package (I really could not see the problem with someone wanting to forfeit half their pay to have a car). Team leaders were only allowed to have standard cars; senior managers could have top-of-the-range cars and executives could have luxury cars. A government-owned water authority did not need to have vehicular status imbedded in its management policy to get better productivity from its employees. I think these days the policy has gone the way of the dodo.

3   Working Together

There are three types of workers: those who get things done, those who watch things get done, and those who wonder how so much got done. - Anonymous

Working together to achieve common goals can be both rewarding and personally satisfying.   Creating teams that work effectively together is an important part of organisational efficiency.   Well-performing teams have the ability to produce awesome outcomes.

The management team at the sewage treatment plant consisted of the plant manager, operations manager, maintenance manager, planning manager, business services manager and the plant manager's personal assistant.   My role as planning manager included managing the capital works program.

My ability to manage the capital works program was a major cause of concern when I was being interviewed for the position.   The plant manager had come from a construction background and had been involved in building the last of the major dams for the city.   He had some concerns about my lack of experience in delivering large construction projects.   I had managed projects before, but never a program, and this was an annual program of $15 million made up of hundreds of projects (admittedly some were very small).

The water authority was notorious for its poor management of the capital works program.   The overall program was more than $200 million a year, with the sewerage group being around half.   The treatment plant was less than a third of the sewerage group, so we were small fry – less than 10%. The main difficulty with delivering the program was that it included a substantial wish list of projects people wanted to undertake, with completely unrealistic timeframes and very little detailed planning. I have always found it frustrating when organisations want projects completed in twelve months and no-one has even started the process of acquiring land, which can take two to five years. Hence the program was almost always underspent.

My role commenced under a new executive regime that was more commercially focused. The accountability in the financial processes had been abysmal. One of the accounting habits was to "dump" operating expenditure at the end of a financial year into capital works projects. This made the operating expenses show a saving, which was politically desirable and, as the capital works budget was never achieved, "spending" more capital money was also desirable.

The business services manager and I worked hard to understand the accounts and get a system in place for tracking the capital forecasts and commitments. She was incredibly competent in analysing and presenting financial information. We would continually challenge each other to improve the financial reporting, and eventually developed a system that was ultimately adopted for the whole sewerage group.

We were trying to reconcile some projects that had been overspent. She interrogated the historical accounting records and found quite a few of those operational to capital expense transfers in previous years. This brought some of the "overspent" projects back under budget and, fortunately for us, someone else had to explain the transfers. Spending time working together had saved us much future angst; explaining project over-expenditures was never a pleasant experience.

One part of the program was the minor capital works managed by the maintenance group. The maintenance manager had a good system for tracking the projects, but the group was continually having difficulties with their requisitions. They were not "good enough" to get approved by the plant manager. He could be quite pedantic when it came to written reports and had earned the nickname "Mr Squiggle" because draft requisitions often came back with more red ink than black. The maintenance staff would often have to do multiple drafts.

One day, the plant manager and I had long discussions about redrafting requisitions (I would score plenty of red ink on mine as well). Firstly, we contemplated the education issue. The senior managers and business services personnel were mostly university educated. The maintenance personnel had generally left school when they were teenagers to undertake a trade. They knew what to do and why it needed to be done. They just did not have the formal education to write Shakespearean masterpieces.

Another example of the education divide occurred when the operations manager, who was a young engineer like me, tried to get the plant operators to manage their own budgets. One day, after the operations manager had spent a few frustrating sessions with the operations staff, the plant manager commented that surely they managed their own household budgets. Someone quipped that it was their wives (they were all men) who managed the household budgets, which was probably very close to the truth. It is always important to understand the skill capabilities of personnel rather than assuming that they can undertake tasks, regardless of how simple they may seem to us.

Then we discussed the issue of style. This related to how the information was structured in the requisition. After some hefty debate, the plant manager and I agreed to make corrections to errors and ambiguities in content but not try to agonise over the style. Admittedly, I did suggest that all future requisitions would be in dot points and he could then "stylise" the requisition as much as he liked! We did agree that it was important to pay some attention to style when the requisition had to be approved at a level higher than the plant manager. This affected very few of the maintenance requisitions.

The maintenance manager and I worked hard to develop some straightforward templates for the maintenance personnel to use when writing requisitions. Together with the business services manager we also improved the minor capital works tracking process. As the management group stared to work together as a team, the plant personnel began spending more time undertaking and improving the way they worked, rather than pandering to our personal idiosyncrasies.

The plant manager was in a difficult position. He had very little experience in managing a sewage treatment plant. The other section managers considered him the least experienced and they took full advantage of this. He would often come back from the section managers' meetings battered and beaten. The other section managers were experts at deflecting issues by criticising his performance.

He relied heavily on the operations manager who, like me, was young and inexperienced. Sometimes the operations manager struggled with timely communication. Once, the plant failed to meet its environmental licence conditions. The plant manager only found out when the divisional manager asked him about the "please explain" letter from the regulating authority. The operations managers had been focussed on trying to fix the problem, but had neglected to tell the management team that it had occurred. The plant manager should have been told as soon as the problem occurred, if only to be prepared for questions from the executive team.

The plant manager was an honest and committed leader, and worked hard to ensure that we were supported in the work we were doing. I remember having a particularly hard week and was irritable and grumpy – as my wife would say "a bear with a sore head". I had been to a few difficult meetings with our project managers and when I returned there was a "Post-It" note with a smiley face stuck to my computer screen. When I asked my team who had put it there, they replied that the plant manager had visited – he had just come to check that I wasn't letting things get me down. Sometimes little things can make a big difference to your day.

We were a good team. We were far from perfect, but we challenged each other, trusted each other and backed each other up when things became difficult. As far as I am aware, we were the first group in the organisation to deliver its capital works program in many years.

◆ ◆ ◆

A well-performing group is one that effectively undertakes its required functions or tasks with a reasonable degree of efficiency. A non-performing group is one that either does not effectively perform its required function, or is grossly inefficient and has difficulties improving its performance. Within an organisation, non-performing teams can operate at management levels, such as at the team level or at the executive level. They can also occur cross the organisation, which can lead to a silo mentality. It is important to emphasise that just because a group delivers its required function or task, if it is inefficient, then the performance of the group needs to be addressed.

There are a number of factors that affect the performance of a group such as clarity of task or function, timeframes, resourcing and operating boundaries. Resourcing includes the access to physical resources and the capabilities of the individuals in the group to undertake the task. An indication that the ineffective management of one or more of these factors are affecting the group performance can present itself in the unconscious behaviour of "acting out".

Individuals and groups do not usually deliberately or rationally behave poorly. However, in order for people to cope with stress and anxiety, unconscious mechanisms can influence the way that they work. This is why attempting to change behaviour is often ineffective – people do not realise or acknowledge that they are behaving poorly!

Wilfred Bion, a pioneer in group behavioural theory, developed the concept of "basic assumption groups" as a way of classifying the "acting out" modes of non-performing groups. In essence, it is the "unconscious behaviour" operating within a group that hinders the group's ability to effectively undertake its required tasks. He classified the unconscious behaviour into three categories; dependency, fight/flight and pairing. While the dependency and fight/flight classifications seem to have stood the test of time, the third classification, pairing, is more difficult to explain and understand, and less often referred to. That does not make it less important.

Dependency relates to a group that continually defers to its leader for guidance as it avoids undertaking the task set before it. It is not the deference to the leader in itself that is the issue; it is the use of deference to not undertake the task. This is the dysfunctional mode often associated with tightly controlled or overbounded organisations.

Fight/flight relates to a group that fights about the nature of the assigned task or ignores it completely. Again, this is not the group that is assertive in seeking to clarify or determine more efficient ways to undertake the task. It is the group that spends its time in incessant debate or undertaking tasks completely unrelated to the required task. This is the dysfunctional mode often associated with "laissez-faire" or underbounded organisations.

The third type has traditionally been called pairing; however, I would prefer to think of this group as "messianic". It is the group waiting to be saved. It is waiting for someone to save the group from the task. It spends its time hoping and preparing for the "saviour", rather than undertaking the task. The irony is that if a "saviour" does appear, he or she is often isolated and excluded from the group as a "misfit". This is the dysfunctional mode often associated with management.

It is important for team leaders to recognise the symptoms attached to each of these non-performing groups and manage the underlying cause, rather focusing on the behaviour.

Here are a few observations I have made over the years regarding effective teams:

- Teams need to understand what their primary goals are and assess themselves against the achievement of those goals.

- Team leaders should be encouraged to show a high level of emotional maturity and work with their team to find out why difficulties occur. Managers who continually criticize team members for not being "team players" or come from the Nike "just do it" philosophy are mostly insecure and incompetent. More often than not it is a lack of clear goals, or competent systems and resources allocation to achieve those goals, which cause behavioural issues.

- Effective teams allow the opportunity for critical assessment of each member's performance and seek continuous improvement of the team's outcomes. A team full of "noddies" (those who always acquiesce to the team leader or try to second guess the solution wanted by senior management) are rarely high performing and are a great risk to the stability of an organisation. It can be much more comfortable managing a team that does what it is told and is reluctant to challenge the status quo – but the team is unlikely to achieve more than average outcomes.

- Communication and communication. And if all that fails there is always communication.

- Good core values of a competent team include honesty, trust and respect. Honesty is not openness. It is appropriate in a work environment to answer a question with "that is none of your business". Openness would require full disclosure, which is highly inappropriate in the workplace when personal matters are involved.

Awesome Outcome Principle:

Extraordinary innovation and awesome outcomes are achieved through extraordinary teamwork.

Encouraging the reluctant soldier into battle!

Matt J

Post Script

Like all good public service teams, the treatment plant management team was disbanded just as quickly as it was formed. The business services manager went on maternity leave. I was keel-hauled into managing the capital works program for the whole sewerage group. The operations manager left the organisation to pursue other interests not related to engineering. The maintenance group was out-sourced and the plant manager took twelve months long service leave.

One of the signs of a productive working environment is the ability for people to join and leave a team without affecting the ability of the team to achieve the required outcomes. Teams should not rely on personality or prescribed behaviour to achieve great things, but on a commitment of the team members to work together to undertake the required tasks in a supportive environment.

However, when a team is completely disbanded, no matter how productive and successful, it is difficult to replicate the teamwork developed. The treatment plant had significant difficulties in integrating the outsourced maintenance team. Even though I was responsible for the overall capital works program, they struggled to deliver their capital works projects. I even succumbed to lowering the estimates from other projects to make up for the treatment plant projects where there was little confidence of delivery. The sewerage division was able to meet the overall capital expenditure plan as long as no-one looked too closely at the individual projects!

4   The Maverick

*"If proposals for change must always be judged feasible
and realistic, we are restricted to modifications of the
status quo" - Gareth Morgan*

When I started at the water authority, personal computers
were a bit of a novelty and the information technology
group was fixated with large mainframe systems. Eventually, the organisation became consumed by the personal
computer culture. Admittedly, this also coincided with a
change in its information technology service provider; a
move to internal information technology strategic development and a newly focused strategy around the previously
disregarded concept of customer service. The most influ-
ential paradigm shift was that the organisation started driv-
ing the information technology requirements rather than
the other way around.

An example of this was the internal telephone list. The telephone list was updated every few weeks and was originally
distributed as a paper booklet, and later via E-mail (still in
the format of a booklet!). The water authority had thousands of employees so there were pages and pages of people on the telephone list. It would take an eternity to find
someone's name on the list.

This was not very efficient; so I wrote a little computer
program that read the telephone list and created a pop-up
box on the computer with the telephone list. The screen
allowed the user to search for a person's telephone number
by name, section or department. It allowed the user to type
in part of a name and then select the name from the list.

While this functionality would be considered standard on electronic devices these days, back then it was revolutionary.

As soon as my team saw the program, they wanted a copy. Then the rest of the section wanted a copy. The program was reconfigured to read the telephone list from a central file on the computer network and we had the receptionist keep the file updated. Eventually we had the most accurate and up to date telephone list in the organisation, and the little program had gone viral.

The information technology department was developing a similar project for the telephone list, but it was a very low priority. When they heard about the little program, they immediately tried to have it banned. This was an extremely unwise move as a number of the personal assistants were using the program. In my experience, some of the most important people in a bureaucratic organisation with whom to foster positive relationships with are the personal assistants. All wise employees know that this is where the real power lies. Mostly it resides in the power of the personal assistant to hinder the progress of action required from an executive manager. It's remarkable how requisitions requiring executive approval take much longer to get approved for people who have little regard for the personal assistant. It's even more remarkable that these same people failed to grasp why it took so long to get their work approved. The personal assistants were always very polite to them!

The challenge was out, and the information technology department moved the telephone list up to a priority project. They created an intranet based telephone list, but it did not have the searching capability of the little program, so the little program was still in wide usage. Eventually, someone from the information technology department decided to come and talk to me about the little program. The little program eventually became redundant and the intranet telephone list became fully functional, inclusive of the functionality of the little program.

To his credit, the information technology department's customer service manager started taking me out to lunch on a regular basis. We would discuss the strategic intentions for technology in the authority – and I tended to get my computer issues solved quickly.

◆ ◆ ◆

There has been much written over the years regarding institutional organisational structure and group behaviour. Some early important work on the behaviour of groups was undertaken by Wilfred Bion, who was a psychoanalyst during the Second World War. Using his work as a basis, organisations can be divided into three groups – the Establishment, the Workers and the Mavericks.

The Establishment are those who are responsible for the outcomes of an organisation. In most traditional structures they are the directors and the executive. The Establishment are responsible for developing the desired outcomes of an organisation. However, they should also take responsibility for making the organisation a safe place to work, both physically and emotionally.

The Workers, for want of a better term, are those who undertake the majority of production. Their role is to undertake the tasks that achieve the desired outcomes. The level of autonomy to undertake the tasks is usually determined by the Establishment.

Mavericks are those people in the organisation who innovate and instigate change. They are rarely comfortable with the status quo. They are always potentially disruptive to both the Establishment and the Workers, but are critical if the organisation is to meet the needs of the changing external environment.

I have always liked the quote above from Gareth Morgan. Organisational rules and etiquette are mostly designed to stabilise the working environment and maintain the status quo. In order to create innovation, Mavericks break "the rules" and disturb the comfort zone of those within the organisation. They work around bureaucratic systems to make outcomes more effective and efficient. Their motto is "it is often better to ask for forgiveness than seek permission". It is important for the Establishment to harness this energy for good, otherwise it can be used for evil, and the Maverick can create significant disruption and damage to the organisational product and culture.

It is important for Mavericks to understand the "big picture" vision of an organisation, and the underlying risks associated within the operating environment. Within that context and some clearly defined boundaries, they can create awesome change through innovative ideas and processes. Without the organisational context, Mavericks can create havoc.

A good example of the role of the Establishment and the Maverick can be seen in the early Christian tradition played out by Peter and Paul in the development of the early church. Peter was a fisherman and had walked and talked with Jesus during his public presence. Peter had been anointed as the "rock" or foundation of the church. He epitomises the Establishment. Paul was a scholar and started life as anti-Christian. Following a supernatural encounter, and together with his deep intellectual understanding of the Jewish scriptures, he gained a genuine understanding of the Christian faith. He became the Maverick – the "outsider" who continually challenged the status quo.

While Peter and his mates hung around the places they were comfortable with, Paul trekked off through Asia with his new found faith, testing it out within the marketplaces and intellectual forums. Peter often fell back into following the traditions he was familiar with, rather than taking his newly found faith and applying the principles to the changing world around him. This often caused a great deal of tension and heated discussion between Peter and Paul. Peter was solid and dependable. He had the character and personality to establish a strong church. Paul was unrelenting and continually challenged the culture of the early church, making sure it stuck to the underlying message, and transforming it into something that influenced people's daily lives.

The Establishment and the Mavericks don't have to like each other, but they do have to find ways of working together for organisations to flourish and meet the demands of an ever-changing world. There is not a lot of evidence that Peter and Paul were great mates, but they did change the direction of the known world.

Here are a few observations regarding organisations and Mavericks:

- It is almost impossible to effectively implement innovation without being a Maverick. Attempting to maintain the status quo while implementing change is nonsense.
- Mavericks will disrupt as organisation. Get used to it and make the most of the opportunity.
- Mavericks are amoral; they can create awesome outcomes or massive destruction. The Establishment are ultimately responsible for ensuring the former rather than the latter.
- The more Mavericks understand the "big picture" outcomes of the organisation, the more likely they are to achieve them.
- Mavericks need encouragement and support, but also need to be accountable for their actions and the organisational outcomes.

Awesome Outcome Principle:

Mavericks enable awesome outcomes by challenging the status quo.

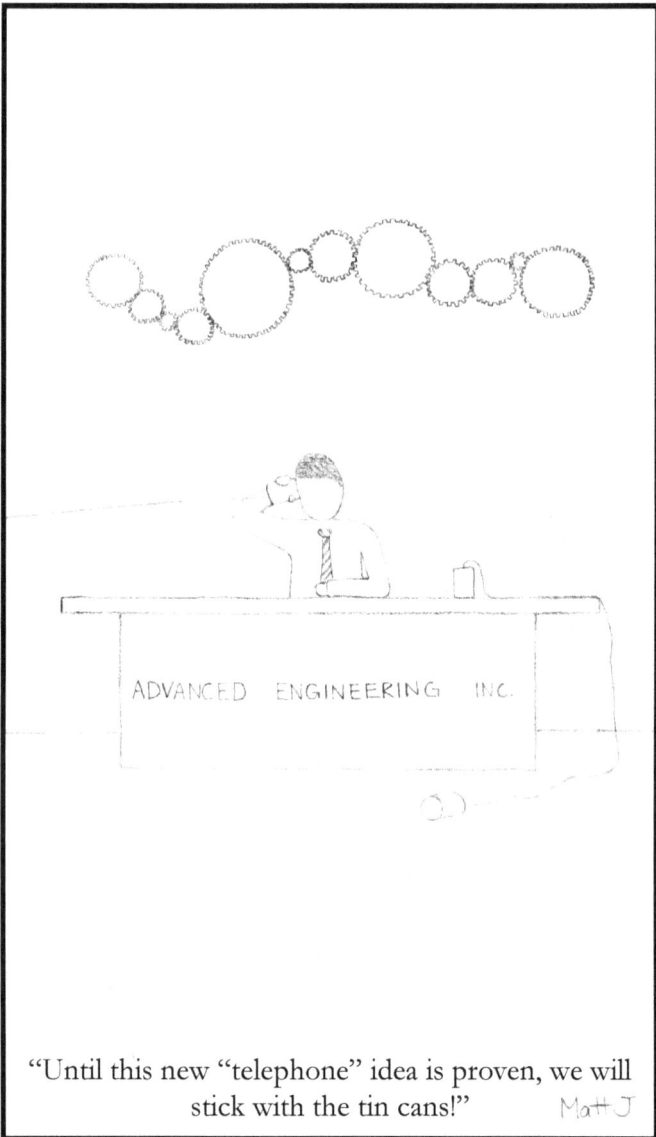

"Until this new "telephone" idea is proven, we will stick with the tin cans!"

Post Script

Years later I was doing some work for an organisation where the information technology department was paranoid about people damaging the integrity of the computer's operating system. They had spent an enormous amount of time and money disabling the capacity for users to get into the operating system from the Windows environment. They had reconfigured the system on every personal computer.

We lost a file on a computer one day and I tried to access the operating system to find it. I couldn't get into the system in the normal way as the access had been disabled, but after a few minutes worked out another way to get into the operating system and search for the file. One manager, who was with me at the time, left the room and came back with the information technology manager. It would be an understatement to say that he was annoyed and demanded to know how I broke through the system.

I showed him how I did it, and he asked if I knew how that method could be blocked. I suggested it was very difficult without rewriting every piece of Microsoft software being used in the organisation.

5   Taking Opportunities

"Often the presence of mind and energy of a person remote from the spotlight decide the course of history for centuries to come" - Stefan Zweig

My home city is sports mad. Most sports are played here in one form or another (excepting perhaps winter sports like skiing as it doesn't get cold enough in the city to snow – this will come up in a later discussion in regards to inappropriate innovation). Even those sports not played here have huge followings. It is a by-product of a rich multicultural heritage.

The most holy of sports stadiums is the Melbourne Cricket Ground or simply "the 'G". It holds just over 100,000 people and is mostly used for cricket and football (Australian Rules). It has also been used to hold significant international sporting events such as the 1956 Olympic Games and the 2006 Commonwealth Games. Apart from sport, it has been the venue for many international music concerts including David Bowie, the Rolling Stones, Michael Jackson, U2 and Madonna. It was the centrepiece of the 1959 Billy Graham Crusade and was visited by the Pope in 1986. The two holiest of days for sports fans are the annual Australian rules football Grand Final and the Boxing Day cricket test.

As a young engineer it was a little awe-inspiring to be part of the team for upgrading this stadium and the arena. The stadium resides within parkland surrounded by residential properties to the east, north and west, and a major railway interchange to the south. When it rains, stormwater flows from the northwest, across the parkland, then underneath the railway yards to a major waterway. My role was to determine how to manage the stormwater for the surrounding parkland and the arena.

Predicting how much stormwater could be collected from the parkland was relatively easy. Working out how it passed under the railway yards to the river was a nightmare. The utility services (electricity, gas and water) had been there for a long time and their locations were not very well documented. Even if there was documentation, it was difficult to find. While digging a trench using an excavator we accidentally dug up an underground power cable. It was one of the main feeders into the city centre and, as it was not marked on any drawings, we were very lucky no-one was injured. The project manager and I were starting to realise that resolving the stormwater issues was not going to be straight forward.

The project manager was one of those rare, brilliant engineers who to this day I consider one of my great early mentors. I often share his stories with young engineers that he passed on to me. He was just so practical. I would spend hours doing calculations to solve some complex hydraulic problem. He would look at what I'd done and pull out some rule of thumb he had developed to check if my solutions made sense. He was very quick to say the answer didn't seem reasonable. He was almost always correct. When I checked my work, there was inevitably some stupid mistake (attention to detail is not my strongest attribute!).

One night an enormous storm passed over the city dumping huge amounts of rain. When I arrived at work, the project manager was not there, and no-one knew where he was. He came in later that morning soaking wet, covered in grass stains. As it turned out, the stadium had been flooded by the storm, and luckily the grass had been cut that day. The storm had flooded many of the changing rooms and the water level was shown by the height of the grass clippings on the lockers. The project manager had been out marking the levels with a thick black permanent marker pen so the surveyors could measure them later.

We obtained the relevant rainfall data from the weather bureau and calculated that the storm event was rarer than a hundred year event. This met our design criteria, so we set the flood levels 300 millimetres higher (just to be safe) and designed the stormwater system to suit.

To this day I am astounded at the project manager's presence of mind to check the levels. By taking the opportunity to record the effects of an actual rainfall event and then being able to show that the event was a suitable starting point to meet the design standard, we saved weeks of theoretical work to justify the building levels to avoid floodwaters.

I have often found that people will argue about the relevance of this calculation or that calculation – but when a physical level can be pointed to, it is hard to argue back. It is always important to calibrate modelled work against real events.

♦ ♦ ♦

Engineers can sometimes get so bound up in the details that they can't see the wood for the trees. I once worked on the design for a concrete tank to be added to three other existing identical tanks that had been built thirty years beforehand. The design came back from the structural engineers with much thicker walls and fifty percent more steel reinforcement. When the increase in size was questioned, we were told that it was "designed to the code". My boss quietly informed the structural engineers that the existing three had stood up for thirty years and asked how it was possible that with better concrete and steel these days the new one needed to be bigger. The structural engineers went back and redid the design from first principles and agreed that the design of the existing tanks would be good enough. The additional tank still stands thirty years later.

"Presence of mind" can be defined as the ability to think and act calmly and efficiently. When opportunities arise, especially in difficult circumstances and emergencies, the ability to think clearly and laterally is paramount. At these times it can be effective to bring someone from outside the situation for a fresh view. An example of this was a spillage incident at the sewage treatment plant.

I was a little late coming to work one day and found that pandemonium had broken out. One of the large ponds that held treated sewage was spilling into the local creek. People were ordering pumps and equipment to try to lessen the amount of water spilling from the pond. I met with the response team and asked them to explain what was happening. It transpired that the water was spilling out through an old abandoned discharge structure and that the water level was still well below the level of the embankments around the ponds. We worked through the problem and someone suggested that some sandbags might fix the spillage problem, at least temporarily.

Presence of mind is an important skill for Mavericks to develop. Often, in challenging the status quo, Mavericks can get stuck on the problem rather than searching for solutions and taking opportunities as they present themselves. Their preoccupation with changing an inefficient process can ignore an obvious solution. I sometimes get so caught up in understanding a problem, especially if it involves a computer simulation, that I do not have the presence of mind to see the simple outcomes!

Here are a few suggestions on having the presence of mind to take opportunities:

- Look at situations from different perspectives.
- Listen to what others are saying. Sometimes the least obvious person may have a profound insight into a situation.
- Visit other organisations and discover how they are approaching similar situations.
- Look for the possibilities of transposing an idea from one work practice to another, even though at first the practices might not seem related.
- Use some of the alternative thinking tools, such as de Bono's "thinking hats", where looking at problems from different perspectives can engender alternative solutions.
- Get people from outside the team and the situation to give a fresh point of view.

Awesome Outcome Principle:

Having the presence of mind to take opportunities when they occur can lead to awesome outcomes.

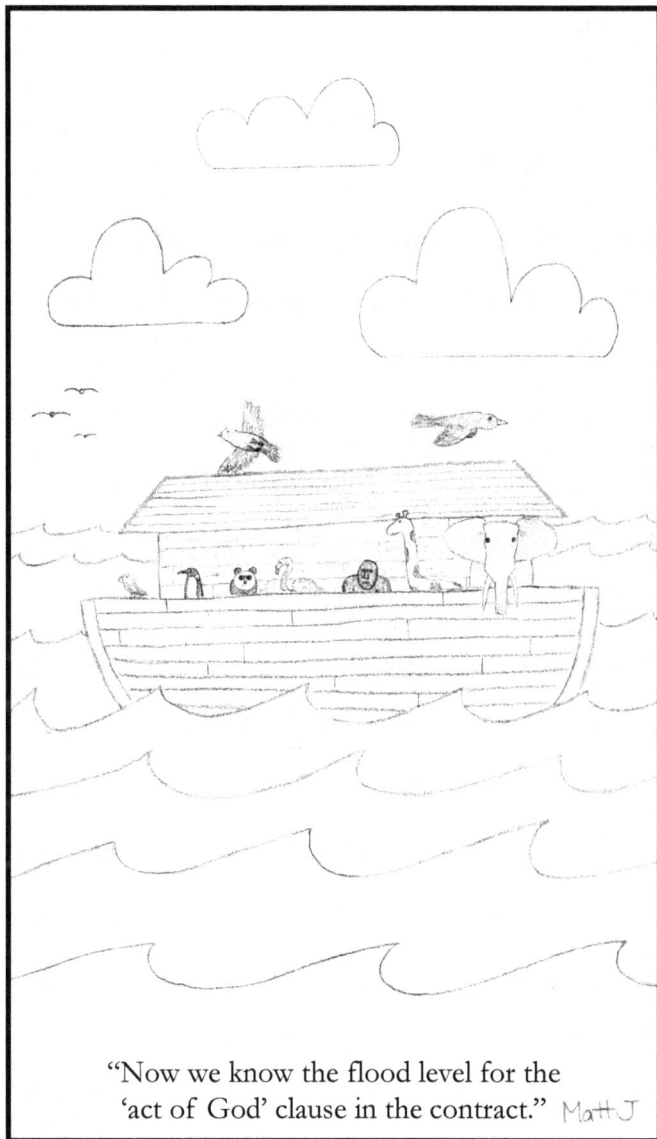

"Now we know the flood level for the 'act of God' clause in the contract." Matt J

Post Script

Quite a bit of stormwater from the parklands ends up at the north east corner of the stadium. The stormwater would usually flow around the stadium to the outlet drain. However, the landscape architects were adamant they wanted a hill between the north east corner and the outlet.

One of the basic engineering principles of hydraulics is that "water floweth downhill" – yes floweth is not a real word but we are engineers! (Thank goodness for spell checkers). So the hill was going to be a big problem. To overcome this problem we designed a very large pipe to go under the hill with a massive bank of entry pits at one end and exit pits at the other. (I wouldn't stand too close if it's raining heavily!)

Alas, I recently visited the ground and saw that my magnificent pits had been removed. The hill was still there, so I wonder where the water from large storm events goes now?

6 Appropriate Expertise

"An expert is someone who knows some of the worst mistakes that can be made in his subject, and how to avoid them." — *Werner Heisenberg*

I joined the water authority just after it had been responsible for one of the worst environmental disasters the city has probably ever seen. Just to be clear on terminology: "sewage" is the liquid that flows in "sewerage", the pipe infrastructure. The appropriate usage is "sewage pumping stations". The phrases "sewerage network" and "sewerage systems" are tautologies. The main reason for towns and cities to have sewerage is to remove human, commercial and industrial waste; minimising health risks and foul odours. Foul smells and health concerns were certainly the reasons given for building sewerage over a hundred years ago in my city.

Sewerage

There are generally two types of sewerage – combined stormwater/sewage systems and separated systems where sewage and stormwater are contained in separate pipes. The advantage of combined systems is that only one network (albeit very large) is required to service a city. The disadvantage is that all the flow has to be treated somehow. As the stormwater flows are intermittent and magnitudes larger than sewage flows, managing the treatment is complex, expensive and often fails during large rainfall events.

The advantage of separated systems is that if the sewerage fails at some point, the systems can be interlinked to allow the sewage to spill temporarily into the stormwater system.

This generally means that the raw sewage ends up in the city's waterways somewhere (creating an environmental issue) rather than out of people's toilets, baths, showers and drains (creating a health issue), which is the lesser of two evils. Most of the time, the water environs clean themselves; people dying from waterborne disease is irreversible.

Although many of the older cities in Europe have combined systems, most modern cities have separate systems. It is generally more cost effective to just treat sewage to meet health and environmental obligations. One of the problems with dedicated sewerage is that stormwater inevitably finds its way into the system because pipes and access pits are poorly constructed or are old and cracked. People sometimes incorrectly (and sometimes deliberately) connect their property stormwater pipework into the sewerage. These are called "illegal connections". The result is that during large rainfall events more than six times the normal sewage flows are required to be taken by the sewerage. The pipe network is required to be sized accordingly, adding much expense to the construction costs.

Environmental Regulations
It would not be economically feasible to size the pipe infrastructure for large infrequent events (more than twenty times the flow) thus the stormwater-increased sewage flow is allowed to spill into the stormwater system. A colleague of mine was working on an evaluation method to determine the effects of sewage spills on waterways. She came up with a good method to work out how often part of the system could spill and still have minimal effect on the environment. However, the methodology was complicated, and would have required the water authority to undertake environmental impact statements where the spills would occur.

This was all too hard for the water authority executive and the senior management at the environmental regulator. As the sewerage had been designed to spill at a lesser frequency of once-in-five-years, the management decided that this was close enough to a one-in-five-year storm event. They argued that this was a good enough performance standard. A non-binding agreement (memorandum of understanding) was developed with the environmental regulator setting the performance standard as the desired goal.

The environmental regulator thought the performance standard was great, mainly because measuring the rainfall events was reasonably easy, so they petitioned the government to make it law through regulation. Now it would be much easier for them to penalise the water authorities if the performance standard was not met. The absurdity of the regulation was that it bore little relevance to the potential environmental damage should a spillage occur. Some waterways can accommodate more frequent spills than others, while some do not cope very well with any spills at all. Generally, the larger waterways are not adversely affected by spillage, while the smaller ones may take a significant amount of time to recover from the sewage spills. Time and money is now spent on "protecting" waterways to meet standards that have little environmental relevance, while waterways that are being damaged have little effort spent on them. Poor legislation and performance standards that are not scientifically credible benefit no-one.

Sewerage Failure

The older sections of the sewerage in the city were constructed over a hundred years ago. Most of it was built by hand using bricks and was constructed in an arch or ovoid (egg) shape. The major sewers are large enough to walk through.

The water authority had been shedding staff and undertaking a series of major organisational restructures and cost reduction activities. A major focus was to reduce its maintenance and operation costs in running the sewerage. One of the innovative operational savings that can be attempted is to alter the way the sewage pumping stations work and create more efficient pumping thus lowering power costs.

The flow in sewerage follows a daily pattern. The flow peaks in the morning and the evening when people are taking showers and preparing meals. It tends to dip during the day and drops to very little overnight. There are a number of factors that affect this, but in general, it takes more than twice the energy to pump twice the flow. If the flow can be evened out during the day, it costs less to pump.

The size of sewers is normally designed to allow for the unwanted ingress of stormwater when it rains. Sewers are generally designed to take more than six times the average daily flow, so when it is not raining, they are mostly empty. The "innovative" idea was to store the peak flows in the morning and the evening in the pipelines and pump them out during the night. Electricity is also cheaper during the evening. Sounded like a great idea!

Many of the brick arch and ovoid sewers were so well crafted, there was little or no cement used between the bricks; they were held together by the arch compression and the pressure of the soil above them. When the sewers were filled during the day, they became pressurised and the bricks moved apart ever so slightly and some of the soil above fell into the sewer.

The process was repeated day and night until huge voids were created above the sewers, edging towards the surface. In some places they eventually came close enough to the surface, mostly where the sewer passed under major roads and were subject to heavy vibration, that the surface collapsed onto the top of the sewer, broke the arch and destroyed the sewer.

This occurred three times within a few months. These were major sewers, carrying the waste from hundreds of thousands of people. Millions of litres of sewage spilled in to the stormwater system every day and eventually made it to the rivers and the bay, closing swimming beaches for weeks during the summer. Not the water authority's finest hour.

During the rectification works on the system, pipes had to be laid on top of roads to divert the sewage and there were major disruptions within the local community. A temporary pumping station and pipeline were constructed along one of the major waterways to divert the majority of the sewage away from the local community. This diversion was not large enough to cope with the flows when it rained, so the pumping station frequently overflowed directly into the river. The environmental authorities were not very pleased about this. The water authority's solution was to spend around ten million dollars on storage tanks.

This all happened just before I started work with the authority. Prior to working for the authority I had worked for a large private engineering consultancy and had been part of the team that had investigated the ingress of stormwater into sewers. I had developed much of the analytical technique and software for predicting the frequency of spillage from sewerage. I applied my knowledge to this situation and determined that the storage tanks would decrease the spillage from around eighty times a year to around sixty times a year. Not a great improvement. There was a large relieving sewer under construction (when I say large, it was a four metre diameter tunnel) that would solve the problem in five years' time. The construction team were adamant that it could not be built any faster.

So the proposed storage tanks were temporary and didn't make much difference to the environmental impact on the waterway. To make any significant difference to the impact on the waterway would have cost hundreds of millions of dollars. Not a good outcome, when that money could have been spent somewhere else to create a permanent environmental benefit.

◆ ◆ ◆

It beggars belief that organisations implement ideas without using the appropriate expertise to analyse the risks associated with them. Or worse still, ignoring the advice of their experts and going ahead with inappropriate innovation regardless.

Unfortunately, this can often be the case when political rather than sound economic or engineering decisions are made or encouraged. Major construction within our city is littered with poor decisions made without using the appropriate expertise to assess the risks undertaken.

One of the worst was the construction of a muti-laned bridge across the mouth of the major waterway that runs through the city. The stability of the ground conditions and the robustness of the construction techniques were seriously underestimated. When major changes were made to the design during construction part of the bridge collapsed. Many construction workers died that day.

Less obvious risks are the increased costs associated with the overdesign of projects. One of the major sewage treatment plants in the city was designed based on treatment plants in Canada. While the design might have been a bargain price, the basis of the design was to allow for sub-zero temperatures and snow. It does not snow in our city, and the additional construction costs were enormous compared to conventional local designs.

This is an area where Mavericks need to take great care, and those watching over them need to have the appropriate governance and checking mechanism to ensure that they do not act outside their expertise. One need go no further than Mavericks who operate in the financial sector on "gut" instinct and the devastation they can cause. Mavericks must learn to develop their own expertise, or find appropriate expertise from others, when implementing innovation in order to create awesome outcomes rather than devastating failures.

So appropriate expertise means:
- Understanding the technical nature of the situation being investigated.
- Understanding the risks associated with how projects are implemented, not just the final outcome.
- Understanding the interaction between economic, environmental and social risks.
- Using local knowledge.

Awesome Outcome Principle:

Using appropriate expertise to review innovative ideas leads to awesome outcomes.

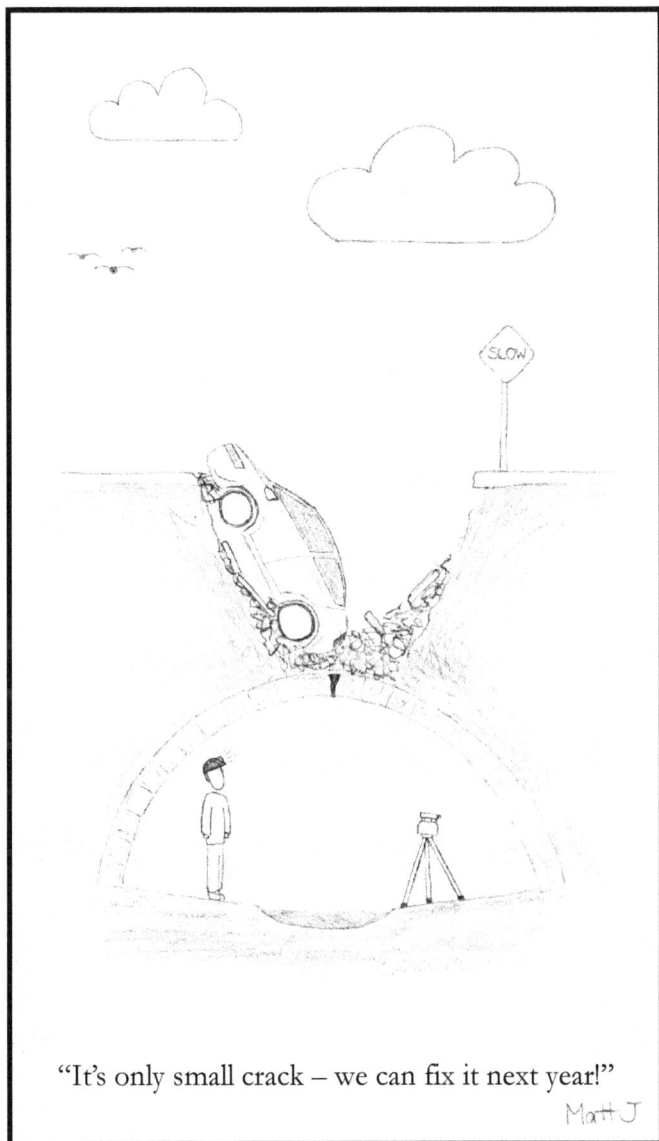

"It's only small crack – we can fix it next year!"

Post Script

The irony of the story is that a few years later I was managing the capital works program, and the construction of the large relieving sewer was part of my responsibility.

The construction project managers had been working on the project for years and a degree of project fatigue had settled in amongst the group. They had become entrenched in their own work practices and were becoming increasing inflexible when it came to changing the program or agreeing to a completion date. There had been a multitude of delays to the project and they were unwilling to commit themselves.

We had come to a major milestone in the project. The tunnel had been completed, and the next stage was to line the tunnel with concrete. After some reorganisation of the project team the relieving sewer was completed nearly a year earlier than was planned.

7   Credibility

"To be persuasive we must be believable; to be believable we must be credible; to be credible we must be truthful."
- Edward Murrow

After working for a number of years with an engineering consulting company, I started work with the water authority in one of their suburban regional offices. Most of the engineers working for the authority had been there since graduation or had come from another water authority. I was an "outsider" having come from private industry and needed to earn some credibility.

The regional office mostly dealt with local water and sewage reticulation and customer connections as well as the larger sections of the stormwater system and the waterways. The local councils were responsible for the smaller stormwater infrastructure.

Stormwater Energy
There was a problem with some stormwater works proposed around a major road interchange. The design engineers had used some complicated mathematics to prove that the stormwater system met the standards. The senior engineer asked me to review the design and, after undertaking some quick calculations, I found that the system had gained energy – which is not possible with a gravity system.

The designer was having difficulties accepting the results. There was a significant construction issue. The contractor had already constructed a portion of the stormwater infrastructure. Much of this would need to be removed and replaced with larger pipes. This was potentially a very expensive process.

The senior engineer decided to engage a hydraulic expert from one of the universities to investigate the problem. After investigating the problem, the expert also concluded that the system had gained energy. The designer was required to revise the design and I had gained a little credibility.

Some of the senior management from head office became aware of my work. The following week a senior position was advertised in the internal recruitment journal. I had only been with the regional office a very short time, so I went to see the section manager to see what he thought about the position. As I sat down, he pulled out the journal - the job advertisement was surrounded by a big black circle with my initials next to it. Despite having just recruited me, he reluctantly encouraged me to apply for the position, which I did. I was the successful applicant.

Computer Networks

During the early 1990s I worked in sewerage planning at head office with about twenty other people. We were responsible for the major sewer infrastructure for a large metropolitan city of around four million people. Personal computers were a reasonably new concept and there was no networking. We shared printers between three or four people with a four-way manual switch box.

The water authority information technology group was very main-frame focused and saw personal computers as a passing fad (and no, they were not IBM!). The building was fully networked for the mainframe terminals, but little thought had been given to the use of personal computers. We were, however, able to connect the personal computers to the mainframe network and operate them as dumb terminals. This did not give us access to printers or plotters. We had asked the information technology staff to create a network for us, but the quote was outrageously expensive.

I had a number of friends who were working in the information technology industry and I asked them why it was so costly to create a network. They were surprised at how much we had been quoted and explained that there was an easier solution. So we bought a couple of cheap network cards to put inside the computers, some cable, plugged it into the mainframe network and it worked fine. (Sometimes it helps to be completely ignorant of things like network protocols!)

We contacted the information technology department to explain that we had found a cheaper solution to creating a network. They came up and had a look, yelled at us for "stuffing up" the network, and went on to explain why it was impossible to connect the personal computer network to the mainframe network.

Never one to be deterred from finding a better way to do things, I had some further conversations with my information technology friends. They explained that the mainframe network provider had just created a software patch that allowed personal computers to run in an isolated network group on the mainframe network. I sheepishly rang the information technology department, gave them the name of a contact at the network company and asked for a quote to get the patches for our personal computers. The total cost of networking twenty computers, a new laser printer and a colour A3 printer was less than one fifth of the original cost quoted previously just for the network. This included the cost of the information technology department's "investigation" to make the system work. This work hadn't gone unnoticed by the senior management.

Eastern Sewage System Strategy

While this was going on, we were doing some real work investigating the major trunk and branch sewers on the eastern side of the city. These were large sewers – three to four meters in diameter and served over two million people. The original plan had been to put very large sewage pumping stations on the branch sewers connecting into the main trunk sewer costing tens of millions of dollars each. To investigate how the system worked, we undertook some extensive monitoring and analysis and found that only one of the branch sewers needed a pumping station. All of the others were fine; this was a huge saving.

We developed a report on the findings and sent it to the relevant section managers. My section manager came to see me a few days later. We had been requested to provide a presentation to the operations group. So we put together all the information onto overhead transparency slides (no fancy projector or large screens in those days). Finally the day came for the presentation. I was nervous at having to present to a group of section managers. The presentation was going quite well, until I began to discuss the prospect of not building the pumping stations.

The operations managers were not impressed. "The plan has always been to build these pumping stations – and no-one is going to convince us otherwise". And the tenor of the conversation degenerated from there, with no resolution at the end of the meeting; just some very angry section managers. It was a disappointing outcome, but we were about to get a lesson on the politics of institutional management hierarchy.

A week later a meeting was held with the divisional managers. I had never met the divisional managers and was very nervous. What I did not realise that my work on the computer network had granted me some credibility amongst the divisional managers. My section manager, to his great credit, had backed my assessment of the sewage system, and was backing me (emphasis on being behind me!) to present to the divisional managers.

The strategy was presented. The divisional managers asked a few very good questions to which we were able to provide some reasonable answers. Then the divisional managers asked the opinion of the operational section managers.

Nothing.

I was amazed. Just a week beforehand these managers had been ferociously opposed to the strategy, and now in front of their divisional managers, they had nothing to say. Welcome to the bureaucratic institution, where the main objective seemed to be maintaining a peaceful status quo with your manager.

So the strategy was approved, and the system is still running the same way twenty years later.

◆ ◆ ◆

Credibility is probably the single most important attribute required to implement new and innovative ideas. The mathematical techniques that we used to undertake the sewage system investigation had not previously been used in the water authority, as was our development and calibration of analytical software based on field measurement. Today, this would be standard computer system modelling; but then it was relatively unique.

Credibility links the concepts of expertise, reliability, and integrity. To be seen as credible, one must not only have the expertise in the area being discussed, but also be seen as reliable when conveying that expertise. Integrity is being able to convey the expertise in a non-partisan way.

One of the difficulties in an organisation is convincing the hierarchy that expertise is not being "spinned" to deliver some other goal, such as increasing budgets or gaining promotions. I have observed this with people seeking to get investment in information technology projects. Selective expertise is used to convince managers of the value of projects, but the reliability of the expertise, when it comes to true implementation cost and times frames, is lacking.

Credibility can also be undermined when the power hierarchy is disturbed, as was the case in this story with the sectional managers. It is critical that, as in this case, senior management seek to use its own independent means to test a proponent's credibility.

A good example of gaining credibility was my time in India. I was helping one of the project workers set up a labour group that could be contracted out to undertake small construction projects. The project worker had a background in theoretical physics and came from southern India. We were working in northern India. There was not a lot of trust between southerners and northerners. The "national" language in the south is Tamil, while the "national" language in the north is Hindi. Needless to say, national government administration is undertaken in English – part of the British legacy. The project manager knew very little about construction.

As the labourers encountered problems with the work, the project manager would ask the labour group leader how to fix the problem. Then he would ask me how I would fix the problem. As the answers I gave generally matched the suggestions from the labour group leader, the project worker began to trust in the labour group leader's expertise in building works and the reliability of his suggestions. As time went on, I was consulted less and less about work issues until I was eventually no longer needed. The labour group leader had gained credibility in the eyes of the project worker.

Credibility is probably the single most important attribute for Mavericks to develop within an organisation. All too often Mavericks want the Establishment to give them a free reign to implement changes with the "just trust me" argument. This is not only irresponsible management by the Establishment, but a foolhardy approach by the Maverick. The Maverick needs to put the effort in to show why their idea is a good one and develop a plan for implementation that manages any associated risks. It sometimes only takes a single failed project for a Maverick to lose all credibility in an organisation.

Credibility is not given, it is earned. This requires:
- Reliability.
- A good track record.
- The appropriate expertise to deliver the outcome.
- A willingness to bring in expertise when required. Asking for help is not a sign of weakness, but prudent management.

Awesome Outcome Principle:

Mavericks require credibility within an organisation to create awesome outcomes.

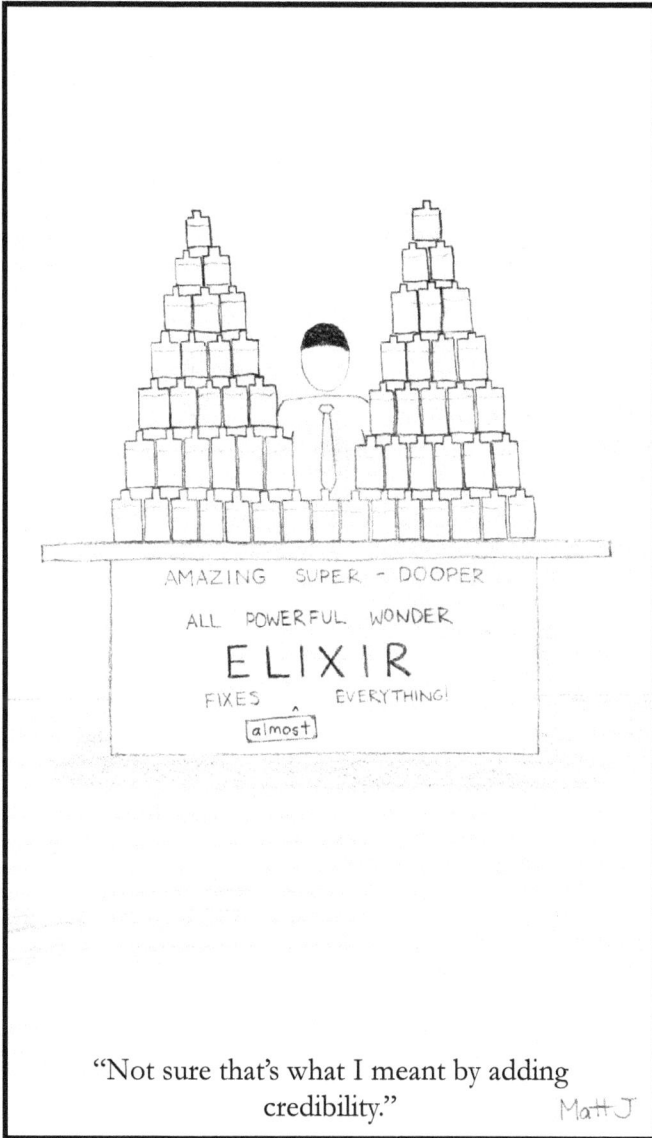

"Not sure that's what I meant by adding credibility."

Post Script

I was young and naïve, and lost some potential institutional allies as a result of the Eastern Sewage System Strategy. A few years later the organisation went through a major restructure. It was split into four separate entities, a "wholesaler" and three "retailers". I was working within the "wholesaler" entity

The "wholesale" organisation was restructured into operational divisions, and as a result of the strategy work I had undertaken, the operational section managers were not happy for me to be a part of their groups.

I was offered a position with one of the "retailers", and it was only the foresight of a divisional manager that it became possible for me to stay with the "wholesaler". He created an opening for me at one of the large sewage treatment plants. It was a very stressful position but one from which I learned much, have fond memories and developed lasting friendships.

8   Robust Discussions

"If two men on the same job agree all the time, then one is useless. If they disagree all the time, both are useless."
— *Darryl F. Zanuck*

The water authority recruited a new Managing Director from the private sector. He was well respected within the manufacturing industry and was brought in to establish robust commercial practices within the authority. Previous Managing Directors had been appointed from large government utilities – the last few had come from the electricity sector. He engaged a new corporate executive team, including an executive finance manager and an executive human resources manager external to the water authority. The executive finance manager was a young, energetic accountant with an almost single-minded obsession with cutting costs. The executive human resources manager was more experienced and had an organisational development approach to people management, instead of the usual industrial relations approach.

The executive decided to move away from the traditional functional approach and restructure the organisation along product lines. Instead of having planning, operations, and project management divisions, we were divided by product; water, sewerage and drainage. In one of my incarnations, I had responsibility for managing the capital works program for the sewerage group. This included managing project expenditure approvals.

Like similar organisations with significant capital expenditure, and a complex bureaucratic approvals process, the cost of the project was estimated somewhere prior to the tendering of the construction phase. For a long time the project cost had been estimated at concept stage, well before any detailed design was undertaken. The estimates were grossly inaccurate and were often referred to as "guestimates". The project managers would be required to deliver the project for the estimated cost. If not, a process not unlike the Spanish Inquisition was undertaken. In order to manage the anxiety created by this process, project estimates were grossly overstated and included very large contingency amounts.

To make the process more sensible, we developed a process of preliminary project approvals. These outlined the business case for the project and assigned expenditure for the investigation, detailed design and tender phase. This would normally be about ten percent of the total project cost. Once a construction cost was determined from the tender phase, a project approval was completed, which included all the costs in the preliminary project approval, the estimated future costs for the project and some contingency for unforseen events.

I had inherited a number of projects that had been developed on the "guestimate" method and two had been seriously overspent. This required the obligatory inquisitorial "interview" with the Managing Director to explain why the project had exceeded its budget. The interviews normally consisted of an intensive grilling, raised voices and feelings of isolation. One multi-million dollar project had gone so wrong that it was more than fifty percent overspent and was the subject of litigation between the water authority, the designer and the constructor. I was given a "get out of jail free card" on that one – the Managing Director was much more interested in speaking to the original project manager.

However, I was required to explain the other project. The divisional manager, for some reason I cannot remember, was not available that day, so one of the other senior managers attended the "interview" with me. The project wasn't greatly overspent and there were some good reasons why the project had changed, so it didn't go too badly – until we started on the topic of contingencies.

The Managing Director was having difficulty accepting the need for contingencies on projects. So we started to have a discussion about the need for contingencies. As I am never one to shy away from a good argument, the discussion became quite animated. I didn't quite understand where he was coming from and he didn't quite understand where I was coming from. He didn't mind a good argument either.

It is worth pointing out that this type of robust debate was not a usual occurrence within a bureaucratic government utility between executives and minions. My background had been in a private engineering consultancy, where robust discussion at all levels was encouraged – it made for better solutions and less legal intervention in the case of unforseen errors!

The poor senior manager, who also knew that I didn't mind a good argument, decided that the Managing Director was probably not someone I should be having an intense debate with. He interrupted the discussion and suggested we leave the topic for another more appropriate time. The Managing Director turned to the senior manager, very colourfully told him to mind his own business, and we continued on with the conversation.

As we debated the issues, it became clear that his concern was that people were using contingencies to "add extras" to project just because there was "room in the budget". My concern was that many projects had unknowns in them, especially if they contained underground components. The cost of removing the uncertainty far outweighed the extra cost incurred if the contingency was used. We came to the agreement that the general "contingency" should be very small (say five percent), but if there were issues that re-quired specific contingency, such as the removal of rock in excavation, a specific contingency for that item only be added to the project. The specific contingency was only to be used if the specific issue occurred. These would be called provisional sums.

Provisional sums are used extensively in contracts to allow for anticipated unknowns or expected problem areas. This assists with getting better tender prices for the client (ten-ders are not "loaded" to cover risks) and a fairer outcome to the constructor.

◆ ◆ ◆

Robust discussion and a clear understanding of issues from all stakeholders, at all levels of an organisation, is a good way to innovate and create awesome outcomes. It can also remove bureaucratic road blocks. This is often not easy to accomplish. Many organisations do not have the emotional intelligence or transitional space to allow these processes to happen. It takes time and effort to transition from one idea to another. Many people in organisations, especially senior managers, are time poor and lack the experience to effectively sift and sort through the relevance of issues within their realm of responsibility. People often respond as the senior manager did in the above story, stifling the discussion and hindering the debate.

A friend of mine shared an example that illustrates how robust debate can be encouraged within a hierarchical organisation. He was in the army reserve and explained how his army unit attempted to encourage robust discussion amongst soldiers and officers of differing rank. When strategic discussions were held, the soldiers and officers would take off their hats and their jackets. These held the insignias of their rank. This signalled that frank and fearless discussion could be held. Once the discussion was completed, they would then all put on their jackets and hats, and the most senior ranked officer would then outline the plan to meet the objective.

A word of warning. If the status quo is challenged within an organisation, and the support of senior levels above the challenge is not guaranteed, it can be a career limiting experience. Individuals that are given the responsibility to implement innovation and change require some protection from the organisation. There needs to be someone with more organisational authority above the individual or group that are affected by the change that is willing and able to step in and protect the change maker from retribution.

This is why it is almost impossible for an internal employee to challenge the status quo at executive level. There is no-one that can effectively step-in. Only a very emotionally mature organisation can successfully provide the protective and transitional space for this to happen.

Social Defence Systems

Emotionally secure organisations that are outcome focused can achieve this safe space, however, many organisations are unable to do this. There is a concept in organisational theory called social defence systems. In order for people in organisations to cope with the stress caused by the workplace, emotionally immature systems are set up, usually unconsciously.

Much of the work underlying this concept has been undertaken within the hospital system. For example, Isobel Menzies Lyth observed that in some hospitals, in order for nurses to cope with some of the horrific conditions of the patients, the nurse referred to the patients by the bed number rather than by their name ("the amputee in bed 6"). This helped the nurses to become emotionally detached from the patients' condition. While this dealt with the immediate concerns, the detachment continued throughout the hospital environment, hindering relationships at all levels in the hospital. This is an example of a social defence system. When the condition starts to spread into other similar organisations, this is known as a social defence fabric.

One of the key difficulties for Mavericks in discussing and implementing change is the imbedded social defence system in many organisations that hinders robust discussion. Challenging the status quo evokes stress and anxiety and many organisations struggle with employees who "rock the boat". Unless these organisations can overcome their own internal defence mechanisms, they are likely to fail when a serious external threat challenges the way they work.

Social defence systems are usually found in the "unwritten rules" within an organisation. They are the way things are done that will never be found in an administrative manual or procedure. However, if they are not followed, it can be almost impossible to undertake effective work.

Here are a few suggestions to be considered when undertaking robust discussions:

- All parties that are a part of discussion need to have respect for each other.
- Realise that once the discussion gets personal, the value is lost.
- Understand that observers of robust discussions often do not understand the interaction and can draw inappropriate conclusions about one or both of the participants.
- Have the courage to disagree with a superior. If the consequence is important, much future angst can be avoided.
- Understand that poorly led and managed organisations can make robust discussion career limiting.

Awesome Outcome Principle:

Creating a safe environment to protect staff from real or imagined retribution allows for meaningful robust discussions.

"What do you mean, "where's my husband" – I'm
the engineer, he is only a doctor!"   Matt J

Post Script

Weeks later, I caught up with the project manager who had been responsible for the project that had gone very wrong. It was a complex project and the fact that it had ended up in litigation between the water authority, the designer and the contractor did not bode well. Ironically it was one of those structures that had been designed for snow!

His interview had not gone very well at all. When I tried to explain the outcome of my discussion about contingencies, he became defensive and told me that he had been directed to only have a contingency of five percent on projects, no exceptions.

Life is always changing. When processes and procedures are cast in stone, and they start to impinge on the ability to deliver awesome outcomes for an organisation, the stones sometimes need to be crushed into sand.

We are often reluctant to ask confronting questions, but they are sometimes the most revealing. One of the questions I use in tender interviews revolves around asking the candidate or contractor when they made a mistake and how they dealt with it. The attitude in the answer is more important than the answer itself.

9 Developing Accountable Relationships

"Compromise is usually bad. It should be a last resort. If two departments or divisions have a problem they can't solve and it comes up to you, listen to both sides and then pick one or the other. This places solid accountability on the winner to make it work. Condition your people to avoid compromise." - Robert Townsend

Developing good productive relationships across organisational boundaries can be difficult at the best of times. The water authority had a projects division that provided project management and construction services for small to medium-size works. They mostly undertook work internally, but also did some work for external clients. There were many private companies that could provide these services, so the authority did not consider the project services division necessary. The water authority had already divested itself of many functions, including engineering design. The division was completely separated ("ring-fenced") from the rest of the authority and contained its own business services functionality, including finance and human resources. The aim of the water authority was to sell off the division as a viable business.

I was working at one of the sewage treatment plants at the time and was responsible for the planning and capital works program. We were required to use the projects division for much of the capital works program implementation. It would be an understatement to say that I had inherited a nightmare.

When I took over the position, most of the projects were running late and over budget. There were significant design flaws in some of them – one was the subject of major litigation. Putting public-service engineers into a private company does not suddenly make them more competent! There were lagoons that were designed with the bases below the water table, so they leaked. There were pumps that caused pipes to literally jump off pipe racks because the pressure transients had not been taken into account. There were covers over channels that were not properly fixed down. When the water level in the channel rose, the covers fell into the channel.

Surviving Earthquakes, but not the Docks

There was a large piece of mechanical equipment that was being fabricated in Kyoto, Japan. During fabrication a devastating earthquake hit the area and the levelled the factory, but the piece of equipment was unharmed. It was checked out and loaded onto a ship and transported to the local sea port. As it was being unloaded from the ship onto the docks, hanging from an overhead crane, the timber frame holding the equipment broke and the equipment smashed onto the wharf. It suffered major damage and had to be sent back to Japan.

I didn't manage this situation very well. The report came back from the projects division claiming it was an "act of God". I failed to see how not securing the equipment properly for lifting by a crane was an "act of God". This caused a major dispute between the project manager, the equipment supplier and myself. Mostly, I was being unreasonably stubborn, but I was also trying to stop the project managers making decisions on behalf of the client without being consulted!

Making Agreements

There was little in the way of formal agreements between the planning group and the projects division for the work they were doing, so we set up internal contract agreements for all the projects. We required them to abide by the costs and time frames of the agreements and also to get agreement from us before any changes were made to the projects. This made them uncomfortable. They had become used to a fairly unrestricted authority to deliver projects, with very little accountability to the end user of the project.

Like all good public service institutions, rather than sort out their issues with me, the project managers complained to their managers and their divisional manager eventually complained to my divisional manager. I was summoned to the divisional manager's office for a "chat". It was explained to me that the projects division was not happy with the way they were being treated. It was also explained to me that the water authority was very keen to sell the division as a commercial operation. It was felt that every time the projects division met a requirement, I changed the rules and kept on making it harder.

I replied that the actual commercial standard they needed to meet was significantly higher than their current performance, but I didn't think they could reach it in a single step. The divisional manager agreed, so it was suggested that I keep on doing what I was doing, but be a bit more pleasant in dealing with people.

Customer Service

Meanwhile, the projects division had decided to engage a marketing manager. I met her for the first time in the corridor of their offices one day. She introduced herself and, after a brief chat, she apologised for taking so long to meet with me. She noted that I didn't seem as scary as the project managers were making out. So we started working together to improve the relationship and the service culture of the division.

A few months later we were having one of our regular catch-up meetings. She said that they had just completed a survey of their external clients, and the issues and comments they received were remarkably similar to the issues I had been having.

The services they provided to our group became the litmus test for measuring performance improvement. There were many more issues and disputes that followed, but we both improved. We became much smarter at being the client and they became better at managing projects.

♦ ♦ ♦

There is a concept that high performing working relationships require all parties to be assertive and co-operative; attempting to satisfy one's own concerns and also satisfying the concerns of others. Where both paradigms are maximised, outcomes can be optimised. In the above example, I needed my work done well, but I also knew that for the projects group to succeed commercially, they needed to change many of their ways of relating to clients. The projects division's aim was to become commercial, but also to meet the clients' needs.

I believe that high performing working relationships can only be achieved when there is a level of accountability within the relationship based on mutual understanding and an innate respect. "Partnering agreements" are sometimes used as an adjunct to contracts in an attempt to improves relationships. These are a complete waste of time. When the contracted works are going well, they work fine. When things start to go wrong, they often fall to pieces. They become an entrenched part of the "blame game". All sides start using the partnering agreement to apportion blame, rather than sort out the responsibilities using the contractual agreements. Personal attacks and power struggles such as "He is not a team player" become the norm.

My observation is that once someone makes a personal attack, he or she rarely have rational grounds to hold their position. At this point there is little value in continuing the conversation.

Contract Management

There is a common view that contract documents should be ignored and only used when something goes wrong ("putting the contract in the drawer"). This is not a view I subscribe to. I once heard an executive manager quote this view, sourcing it from a well-respected engineer in relation to a project I had worked on. The engineer had been one of my managers when I had worked for a large consulting engineering company. In setting up the project, we had spent a significant amount of time writing a contract that was equitable to the both contractor and the client while protecting the integrity of the outcomes required. The highly experienced and well-regarded contract manager on the project referred to the contract constantly throughout the construction, and it was a very successful project (although it was joked one day that it would be pistols at dawn between the contract manager and the construction manager!).

My approach to contracts is very simple. A contract is an agreement between two parties; one party to undertake some work and the other party to pay for it to be done in a timely manner. It should not contain clauses that either party would never invoke. It should not contain clauses and penalties that an organisation would not inflict on its own staff or ask them to undertake tasks that they as an organisation would be unwilling to do. This is unethical. It should not be unbalanced in such a way that one party has significantly more rights than the other party. Both parties should be willing to, and have appropriate systems in place, to abide by the agreements described by the contract. I have often seen contracts with ridiculous payment clauses that neither the client nor the contractor has the ability to adhere to.

Here are a few suggestions for developing good working relationships:

- Clearly define the requirements of each person in the project. Clients need to be clear on what they are asking others to achieve.
- Have a realistic understanding of time and cost requirements.
- Be Honest.
- Deal with each other in a respectful manner. Be professional in dealing with others. Deal with the issue at hand, and do not let personal opinions influence decision making.
- Not be afraid of having robust discussions. Having a good passionate argument early in a project can pave the way for excellent working relationships later on.
- Don't compromise on outcomes, the best that can be achieved is mediocrity – collaborate and urge each other to create awesome outcomes.

Awesome Outcome Principle:

Developing strong accountable relationships based on mutual understanding and respect is paramount to creating awesome outcomes.

"It was him!"

Post Script

I was eventually engaged to manage the capital works program and maintenance services contract for the entire sewerage division. The team undertook some very innovative projects with the projects division, and implemented radical process and contract regimes, some of which I will discuss later. I firmly believe that we would not have been able to make these organisational changes together if we had not had our baptism of fire. The projects division was eventually sold off and we continued using their services for years afterwards.

It is difficult to explain how unusual my position was in the organisation. The divisional manager allowed me a significant amount of leeway to undertake my work. He was willing to be challenged and supported what I was doing. I am sure that at times he compromised his own position within the organisation by supporting me. My colleagues in other divisions did not have the same sort of freedom, and sometimes struggled to create significant change.

10   Middle Managers

"If sufficient number of management layers are super-imposed on top of each other, it can be assured that dis-aster is not left to chance." - Norman Augustine

I have discussed three groups that operate within organisations – the Establishment, the Workers and the Mavericks. In larger organisations there is a fourth group, the Middle Managers.

Why Middle Managers?
In some discussions held by organisational theorists there is the notion that Middle Managers are not helpful, and that a "flat" or matrix organisational structure should be sought after. While this can seem like an efficient way of working, it is often incompatible with the way humans think and work.

As a teenager I was part of a leadership team for the local church youth group. The leadership team was very diverse. It consisted of university students studying medicine, engineering, teaching and the arts. It also had some young office administration workers, trades apprentices and shop assistants. It didn't take long for us to realise that breaking the youth into groups of six to eight for discussions and activities was very effective, regardless of the experience or the level of education of the group leaders. However, sometimes there were not enough leaders present, and the groups became larger and much more difficult to manage. I remember being the only leader present one evening, and resorting to a very dictatorial method of leadership – bush dancing, which, like square dancing or line dancing, is a very structured way of organising people to have fun, while taking away their freedom to act or behave differently!

Physiologically, we can manage around four to eight relationships effectively. Once groups become larger than this, we tend to categorise people into manageable parcels. It is important to understand that if groups are not divided with regards to work structure, they will divide on some social construct (men/women, old/young, and so on), with the propensity for organisational cultural prejudice developing over time. It is hard enough to manage an endemic "silo" culture, where workgroups are confined and find it difficult to relate to each other – but nearly impossible to manage recalcitrant social culture.

An example of poor structure was an organisation that believed that it should only have six levels of hierarchy. This ended up with me being required to manage thirty people as direct reports. At the same time they were introducing balanced scorecards for individual performance, which required weekly reporting on all direct reports. This was completely unmanageable. There was a significant amount of work time devoted to "us" and "them" conversations. I ended up dividing the staff into workgroups with a more senior "team leader" in each group.

Conversely, groups that are too small are likely to not have enough diversity to maintain and develop a critical review of the group's performance.

Work Group Size
I tend to use the "6 + 2" principle for work groups. Any level in an organisation should have up to six direct reports and up to two specialists. It should aim to have at least six

total reports, and definitely not less than four. The "specialists" might be a personal assistant, technical expert or organisational/operational expert. These people are there to assist with the administration of the group, setting group agendas, strategic planning and cross-group technical advice.

Some people are brilliant technically or have superb analytical organisation skills, but struggle to manage people. They don't like managing people and it generally makes them extremely anxious, which can become infectious. There is often the fight/flight response; they either avoid interacting with their staff, or are dictatorially belligerent. Many organisations have difficulties placing these people. Their skills are highly valued. However, many management structures only reward personnel in accordance to the number of people they manage, rather than their value to the organisation. Hence, I generally like to allow for a technical or organisational specialist in each team at each level. The worst thing that can happen is to give these technical experts people to manage to meet the requirements of the salary structure.

If we assume uniform organisational structure (standard equilateral pyramid), we get "right sized" organisations. The smallest being 4 to 8, then 25 to 50, 150 to 300, 800 to 1600 and so on. This is one of the reasons why some organisations struggle to grow. Once it gets to 10 people, it quickly needs to get to 25 to be efficient. The same at 50, it needs to quickly get to 150 to be efficient, and hence the development of middle management to organise the implementation of the Establishment's objectives. The numbers change for skewed organisations, but the principle remains the same.

As discussed earlier, if the members of a group have to manage too many relationships, it is likely to split along social or emotional lines, and become inefficient. There are always exceptions, but my observation is that the principle generally holds true. Keeping groups around 6 to 8 members is normally the best outcome.

What do Middle Managers do?

Generally, it is the Establishment's role to set strategy and business direction. It is the Middle Manager's role to develop procedures and processes which enable the implementation of the organisation's strategic direction. Middle Managers also tend to manage resource allocation, and measure the performance of the organisation against its strategic direction.

The use of a management hierarchy often causes the problem known as "the Peter principle". The selection of a person for a promotion is based on the person's performance in his or her current role rather than on the abilities required to undertake the intended role. Thus, people only stop being promoted once they can no longer perform effectively, and "managers rise to the level of their incompetence".

In the past, middle management was seen as the stepping stone to senior or executive management. However, with the constant restructuring of organisations and the importing of executive management from other industries, this is often no longer the case. This tends to exacerbate the condition known as "middle manager squeeze".

The Middle Manager Squeeze

Middle Manager squeeze occurs when the demands of the Establishment are inconsistent with the demands of the organisation as a whole. This can create a sense of powerlessness within the middle management and sets up a catatonic work ethic which impedes the progress of innovation and change. This is often the case with resource allocation. The demand of the organisation for more resources to undertake tasks while the Establishment seeks to cut production expenses. It can also present itself in other destructive ways as well. I am often reminded of the joke, "Why do grandparents and grandchildren get on so well? – they have a common enemy!" This is often how middle managers feel within an organisation – enemies from above and enemies from below.

An example of this was the development of the strategic direction for one of the major treatment plants at the water authority. We had estimated that the project works were going to cost more than $100 million. However, sometime earlier, the executive had discussed the cost of the project with the Board and suggested that it was less than $100 million. Even though there had been a change in executive since the original discussion, they were reluctant to take the new project cost to the Board.

The divisional manager was in a real bind. While he was trying to meet the needs of the executive, one of his recalcitrant staff (who shall remain nameless!) was adamant that the estimates were not going to change – there was already a feeling that the project costs were on the low side. A "corrected" Board strategy was received from the executive with the estimate crossed out and the old cost written in. As the recalcitrant staff member stormed down the corridor towards the manager's office, there was a desperate plea from the manager – "Calm down, don't worry about this, I will deal with it". He had received the "corrected" paper as well.

Managing egos and personal idiosyncrasies within organisations is difficult at the best of times, but nearly impossible for the Middle Manager dedicated to improving organisational outcomes.

My worst experience occurred when I was employing staff to manage teams in a large organisation. I had arranged for my team leaders to interview potential candidates and come back with their recommendations. I interviewed the three selected candidates and thought they would fit into the group well. One was external to the organisation, one was an in-group promotion and the third was from another part of the organisation. The last step was to get approval from the senior manager.

Unfortunately, the senior manager had heard that the candidate from the other group was a "troublemaker" and didn't want her in the section. I had a further discussion with the candidate and with their manager. There had been some conflict within the group that had not been resolved. However, after more discussion with the candidate and my other team leaders, we were confident that we could work with the person within our group.

The senior manager was unconvinced and I was directed not to employ the candidate. I then had to explain to the candidate that they were unsuccessful and I had to explain why. What do you say to a candidate that meets the performance requirements for the job, was the best candidate for the position and was accepted by their potential colleagues? The Middle Managers' conundrum – do you have integrity and explain the outcome to the candidate, or be economical with the truth and protect the senior management. How do you manage this in an organisation that drills integrity as one of its core values?

This is the Middle Manager's squeeze. It is a difficult situation, and the more middle managers are economical with the truth and protect the senior management, the better they get at it. This creates significant organisational risk as the middle managers become reluctant to express difficulties within the organisation. This phenomenon has been well documented in events prior to the explosion of the space shuttle "Challenger", which I will discuss in more detail later.

Unfortunately, ethical Middle Managers often do not survive in some organisations for very long.

Awesome Outcome Principle:

Appropriate structures that enable good communication are required to maintain awesome outcomes.

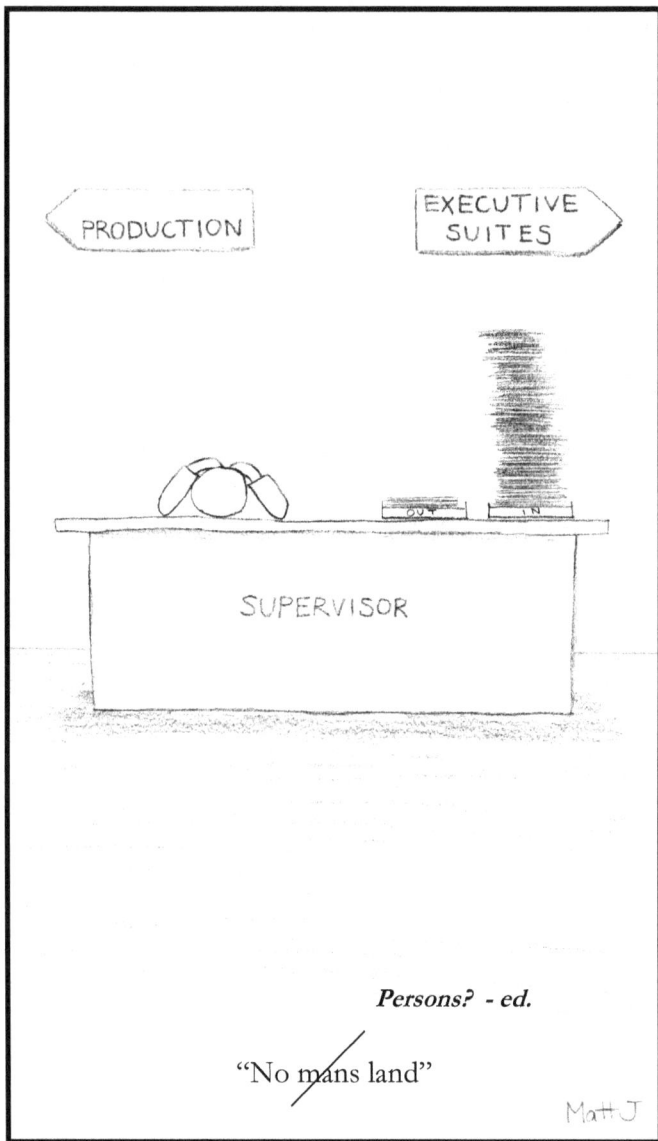

Post Script

The implementation of organisational structure has been effectively used in civilisations for thousands of years. The ancient Roman Empire is said to have lasted for a thousand years, depending on historical perspective. However, the period often referred to as Pax Romana was a long period of relative peace and stability experienced by the empire in the first and second centuries A.D.

One of the main aspects of its stability was the effectiveness of the army. Centuries of warfare had led to the establishment of Legions, consisting of a notional 6000 soldiers (though usually less). Each legion was made up of up to 10 cohorts. Cohort's consisted of 6 Centuriae. Centurion's had 10 Contubernia, which in turn had 10 soldiers. Not surprisingly this is similar to the modern Army Division.

11   Bounded Systems

There is an apocryphal story about a government organisation that was taken over by a larger government organisation. The rationale for the take-over was political, not functional. The smaller organisation had significant cash reserves and the government of the day was in financial difficulty. It was rebranded with the larger organisation's name and the employees effectively changed employer over a weekend.

To help the newly acquired employees feel welcomed into the larger organisation, the personnel department went into the offices of the smaller organisation over the weekend and placed branded ceramic coffee mugs and a small welcome package on everyone's desk. The employees from the smaller organisation were already unhappy about the take-over. When they arrived on Monday morning they did not take too kindly to what they felt was an invasion of their personal space. As a group they picked up their coffee mugs and headed to the roof of the building. Once there, they smashed the mugs onto the car park two story's below.

A coterie of the disaffected staff managed to stay together in the organisation for years. They were destructive and resistant to any kind of organisational change. The individuals were often targeted by management for their "poor" behaviour. Eventually, an external consultant approached this as a systems issue rather than an individual behavioural issue. He worked with the disaffected employees and the organisation as a whole. He encouraged both the organisation and individuals to recognise and own the historical context and then move on. Only then was the performance of the disaffected personnel able to improve.

My understanding of the effects of organisation structure on individual behaviour can be summarised as follows:

Disruptive behaviour and underperformance of individuals and groups within an organisation is often due to inappropriate structure and dysfunctional organisational culture rather than individual behaviour.

Seeking to change an individual's behaviour is a fool's errand and, in a dysfunctional or worse pathological organisation, it is likely to be counterproductive. The behavioural modification process can reinforce rather than resolve organisational cultural problems. At a team level this can be seen when a "disruptive influence" is removed from the team, only for someone else to take on the disruptive role.

To implement innovation and change, it is important to understand something of the organisational context surrounding containment and boundaries. Organisational systems are both physical and psychological. While the physical boundaries in an organisation are reasonably easy to determine (time, task and physical territory), the underlying psychological forces affecting behaviour are often not quite so transparent (emotional territory).

In this context, how "bounded" an organisation is refers to the fluidity of the physical and emotional boundaries within the organisation. If the boundaries are too tight (overbounded), productive energy is constricted, making the organisation inflexible. If the boundaries are too loose (underbounded), productive energy is diluted and dissipated, making the organisation ineffective and inefficient.

Clayton Alderfer identified eleven variables to describe the boundedness of organisations. These six are the most relevant and assessable (to be honest I don't fully understand them all!):

- Goals
- Authority relations
- Role definitions
- Communication patterns
- Unconscious behaviour
- Time span/economic conditions

I will discuss each of these variables in relation to a well-bounded organisation and show how some organisations, like the water authority, can have dual bounded structures operating within the Establishment and the Workers.

Goals

There are two important aspects to understanding goals set by an organisation – clarity and consensus.

An underbounded organisation will have unclear goals without consensus. Competing goals are often not linked to the organisation's required outcomes and a sense of meaninglessness and frustration is often felt throughout the organisation.

An overbounded organisation will have clear goals, but this can often be attached to an ideology or "religious" fervour not specifically related to the environmental context in which the organisation operates. At one stage the water authority was in a cost cutting phase, but the goal to improve efficiency had been attached to the ideology that outsourcing work to private contractors was more efficient than undertaking the work internally. I reviewed the efficiency of the last remaining internal maintenance groups at a large wastewater treatment plant. They had already outsourced those tasks which they could not do efficiently, and I saw little value in outsourcing the remaining work. The executive disagreed and outsourced all of the work because "there are always efficiency gains when work is undertaken by contractors". Needless to say the efficiency gain were never fully realised.

A well-bounded organisation will have clear goals and objectives that meet the external environmental needs that affect the operation of the organisation. It will generally have consensus within the organisation's internal community.

The water authority had a complex corporate plan that set out detailed goals and objectives (overbounded). There was a dedicated group of people up in the heights of head office, close to the executive, who developed this plan every year. However, I don't think I ever saw the plan or was part of its preparation, and I was in the planning group! We generally set our own projects, or were led by the needs of the operations group. Sometimes we were distracted and fixed the computer network! Classic underbounded at the Worker level..

Authority Relations
The major role of the Establishment is to define and adjust boundaries to allow efficient and effective work to be undertaken.

In an underbounded organisation, the authority relations are fragmented and unclear. Accountabilities are often multiple and conflicting. These organisations spawn "Teflon" managers, who are adept at taking credit for all the positive achievements while making sure that none of the failures stick. There is often significant disquiet amongst the staff and much energy goes into "protection" mode, rather than addressing the required tasks.

In an overbounded organisation the authority relations are highly centralised. There is little room for creativity and innovation, or feedback to allow correction for impending disasters. There is an apocryphal story relating to the sinking of the British fleet in 1707 off the Isles of Scilly. It is alleged that one of the sailors suggested that the fleet was not in the position determined by the navigator. The navigator took offence and the sailor was hung for insubordination. Not long after the fleet struck rocks and four of their ships were lost.

In a well-bounded organisation, the Establishment provides enough leadership to allow the organisation to achieve the desired outcome, with appropriate feedback loops to manage risk.

Within the water authority the relations were very hierarchical with a strict, bureaucratic approval process. However, mechanisms for checking how the budgets were spent were poor or non-existent. Prior to heading on vacation, my manager put some folders on my desk, just in case someone needed any information – but assured me it was nothing important. When I looked, it was a multi-million dollar upgrade for a sewage pumping station. I rang a few people to find out how it was going. The answer was not so good – late and over budget, and the operations division was very unhappy. But there no adequate tracking or reporting process and the accountabilities crossed divisions.

On paper, the planning group were responsible for the capital works program, but that was not how the reporting arrangements operated; very underbounded.

Role Definitions

Expectations placed on individuals often determine role behaviour in an organisation. The clarity and consistency of the role definition is a key to boundary management. Tension is often caused when there is disparity between the expectations of management relating to staff performance and role definitions.

In an underbounded organisation role expectations are unclear and conflicting. People feel fragmented, conflicted and isolated. Much unproductive time is spent trying to determine what is required to be done.

In an overbounded organisation roles tend to be highly precise, detailed and restrictive. People feel confined, constrained and restricted, with little scope for creativity or innovation. Collaboration between staff is difficult to obtain, and more often than not a destructive competitive culture pervades the organisation

A well-bounded organisation will tend to have outcome based role definitions that provide clear guidance on the outcomes required, but allow for innovation and ingenuity in how those outcomes are achieved.

The water authority had position descriptions for all roles within the organisation; however, these were mostly used to justify staff numbers. They were detailed and very prescriptive in the way they were developed (overbounded). However, they were very rarely referred to and the work that individuals undertook often bore little resemblance to their position description.

Communication Patterns

Effective communication within organisations is key to its efficient and effective functioning.

In an underbounded organisation chaos and disorganisation are common with an underlying lack of confidence and feeling of futility. The balance of feeling is generally negative and pessimistic. Communication is often conflicting and unrelated to the needs of the organisation.

In an overbounded organisation negative feelings are stifled. Criticism and negativity are repressed, and the balance of feeling is positive and optimistic. Thus critical communication rarely occurs and risks are poorly managed.

A well-bounded organisation has clear, undistorted communication with robust feedback loops. The message sent by the Establishment is the same message sent by the team leaders. There is a balance between positive and negative feelings, optimism and pessimism.

The executive at the water authority were basically invisible to the general employees. They were rarely seen or heard from, and fear was the common feeling when summoned to the executive offices. However, undertaking projects and tasks required meeting the needs of multiple stakeholders and chaos ruled supreme.

Unconscious Behaviour

A well-performing group is one that effectively undertakes its required function or task with a reasonable degree of efficiency. A non-performing group is one that either does not effectively perform its required function, or is grossly inefficient and has difficulties improving on its performance. As discussed previously in the chapter on Working Together, the unconscious response to anxiety and stress can cause groups to "act-out" in ways to avoid undertaking the required tasks.

An underbounded organisation will generally "act-out" in fight/flight unconscious behaviour. There will either be continual conflict, often around non-task related issues, such as who gets the window seat, or passive aggression, such as when my children use the term "whatever"! Decision making revolves around minimising the internal conflict (both passive and aggressive).

An overbounded organisation will generally "act-out" in dependency unconscious behaviour. Individuals in groups show little or no initiative, and those who show initiative are quickly "squashed" by the group. Decision making revolves around minimising accountability and possible retribution.

In well-bounded organisations tasks and functions will generally be undertaken in an efficient and effective manner. Decisions will be made in a rational and conscious manner. There will always be recognised room for improvement and a performing group will generally continuously improve the delivery of its function or task.

The water authority favoured dependency within the management and fight/flight amongst the staff. The behaviour of the senior managers in the example used in the chapter on credibility bears this out. When the senior managers were within the organisation, they were more than ready to argue and be critical (fight mode), but very quickly went into dependency mode when faced with the divisional managers. This was not flight mode. Once the senior managers were told what the outcome was, they were willing to let the process continue. If it had been flight mode, there would have been a degree of passive obstruction.

Time Span/Economic Conditions
The time horizon in which an organisation operates is often an indication of its boundedness. A closely related concept is economic conditions, or taking the concept more broadly, the operating environment. I have linked it with time span because it has to do with the nature of organisational stability and the management of crises, which often play out in relation to an organisation's view of time.

An underbounded organisation is beset by the "tyranny of the urgent". It doesn't have time to plan and, while it is more effective at dealing with crisis and environmental change, it is usually very inefficient. There is often a sense of "déjà vu" as the same sort of organisational crises keeps reappearing. In a telecommunication organisation, the market and products are continually changing and competition is fierce. These organisations tend to be very short-term focused. As they drift into becoming underbounded they have poor governance and do not develop adequate processes and systems to manage their risk. They often get themselves into financial difficulties and have problems creating a safe working environment for their employees.

An overbounded organisation is fixated on the long term and often has difficulties dealing with real crises and changes in the operating environment. Where an organisation has a safe revenue stream, such as a government run water authority with a monopoly customer base, it will tend to deal with work planning on a long-term work horizon. As it drifts into becoming overbounded, it tends to see the short-term customer issues as irrelevant, which is often its undoing. The customer eventually gains a voice through the political process.

A well-bounded organisation has a long-term view of its viability, but deals with the short-term issues as they arise and has good risk management and contingency planning.

The economic environment for the water authority was very stable. It was a monopoly with a fixed customer base, low growth and the ability to change its pricing to meet its operating costs. Its major assets required long-term planning and it was required to deal with daily system issues. This was the external environment seen by the management. However, the internal environment ran in crisis mode, with cost cutting and short-term economic gains a priority, to the detriment of long-term planning. Massive redundancies led to staff insecurity and an unwillingness to take risks to improve productivity or performance. While notional productivity gains were made, there were catastrophic consequences, such as the major failure of the sewerage discussed in the chapter on expertise.

Conclusion

To gain effectiveness in productivity and deliver awesome outcomes, an organisation should be well-bounded. Overbounded organisations are generally effective at the task at hand, but rigid in response to change and innovation. Underbounded organisations can change rapidly and be innovative, but lack the discipline to implement effective change and innovation without placing the organisation at significant risk. The bounded position for each organisation depends on the environment the organisation works in. A long term, asset rich water authority will tend to err on the overbounded, while the high-tech modern telecommunications organisation will tend to err on the underbounded.

However, it is possible for the Establishment to operate in one mode (usually over-bounded) and the Workers to operate in the other mode.

This was the case when the Managing Director from private industry took over the management of the water authority. When he came in, he spent time with the Establishment (executive and senior management) and determined from their discussion and behaviour that the organisation was overbounded. As shown in the examples above, this was not the case.

There has been significant research undertaken in regard to overbounded organisations and the concept of empowering teams to determine the way in which outcomes can be achieved. Less is understood about underbounded organisations and even less about the overbounded/underbounded Establishment/Worker conundrum. What is recognised is that if an empowerment regime is attempted to be implemented on an underbounded organisation, the risk of organisational failure increases. In order to manage the organisational risk, a stricter form of governance and control is required. Where the Establishment is overbounded and has failed to ensure that the appropriate governance and control mechanisms have filtered down into the organisation, the organisation may need to become more overbounded before it can become well-bounded.

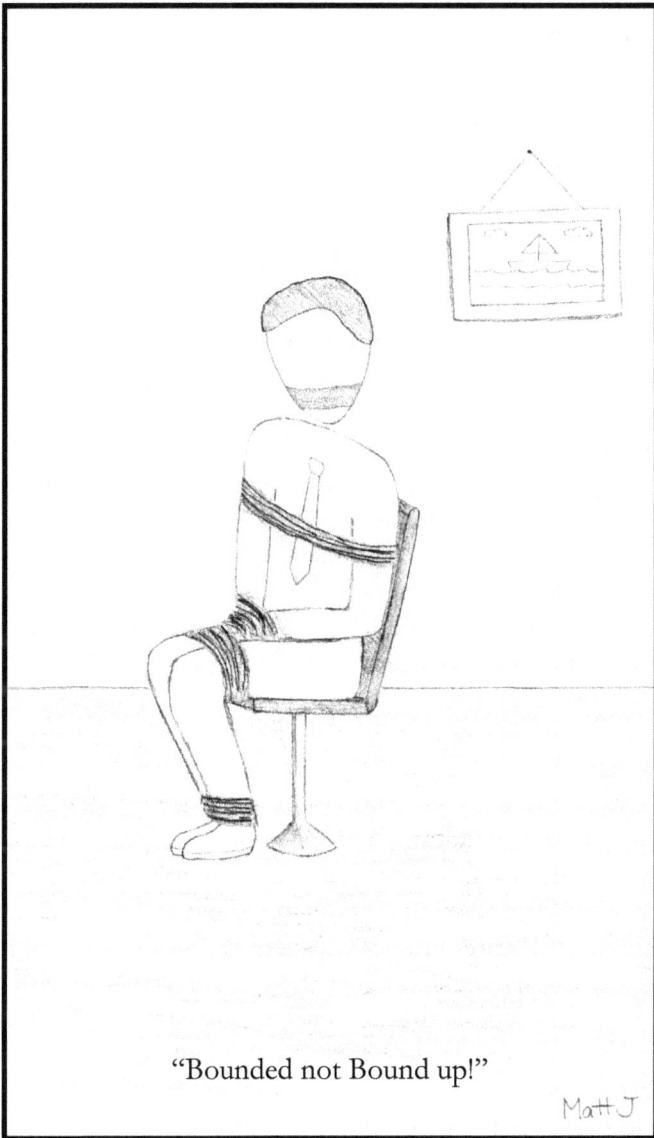

"Bounded not Bound up!"

Matt J

12   The Model

Organisations require some form of structure to operate. I struggle with the anarchic position of the post-modernists and their call for the devolution of organisational structure. While I find the deconstructive nature of their approach to organisations very helpful, people need clear objectives and boundaries to effectively work and relate with each other. This implies some form of structure within a power-sharing paradigm. While poor structure can be extremely detrimental to both organisational and personal health, the absence of structure is hardly a remedy for this.

I was once involved in an organisation that was highly structured, had a diverse membership of culture and personality types, but was probably lacking in gender balance and distributed age profile. Members of the organisation were encouraged to be dedicated to the organisation's goals, but also to deepen their understanding of the underlying principles that gave reason for the organisation's existence.

The organisation grew rapidly and started to break into groups based on culture and personality types. These groups became more formalised and in the process the organisation became less and less diverse, and less tolerant of difference and criticism. The focus moved away from deepening the understanding of the organisation's underlying principles to a more accommodating and superficial view of its heritage. Eventually some members of the organisation became less tolerant of the structure and a spilt occurred between the conservative members and those with a post-modernist approach. While the organisation still operates, it is a shadow of its former existence, with its relevance to its surrounding environment ever diminishing. I don't think the post-modernist faction still exists.

Throughout this book I have discussed the concepts of the Establishment, the Workers, the Middle Managers and the Mavericks. In this chapter I will outline a model, based on my research and experience, to create a structured environment that is conducive to innovation and the creation of awesome outcomes.

Organisational Roles

At a simplistic level, the roles within organisations can be summarised as follows:

- The role of the Establishment is to set the strategic business direction and monitor the outcomes.
- The role of the Middle Manager is to manage boundaries, workgroup containment and resource allocation.
- The role of the Maverick is to challenge the status quo, encourage innovation and provide a pathway for continuous improvement.
- The role of the Worker is to deliver the required outcomes.

Traditional organisations are structured around the Establishment, the Middle Managers and the Workers, with a tolerance for Mavericks scattered throughout the Middle Management. This allows for pockets of innovation to occur throughout the organisation, but is highly reliant on the quality of the Establishment to encourage and support the Mavericks together with ability of the Middle Management to tolerate disruption, criticism and change.

More enlightened organisations recognise the value of Mavericks and assign places within the structure to accommodate them. This can be in the form of special project teams or strategic planning groups. These groups sometimes fail as they move the focus from facilitating change to seeking to gain control of the Middle Managers and Workers. This is a major failing of many information technologies "solutions".

More draconian organisations do not tolerate the Mavericks at all – they are completely absent or repressed. These organisations often have very short life spans or, if they are perpetual bureaucracies, become oblivious to the destructive impact they are having on the surrounding environment.

Power and Change

While structure is often the mechanism for the distribution of power and control within an organisation, the appropriateness of the structure, and how well the Mavericks are accommodated, will greatly influence the ability of organisations to implement innovation and create awesome outcomes.

The diagram below illustrates the relationships between the organisational roles with regards to the desire for control and the appetite for change.

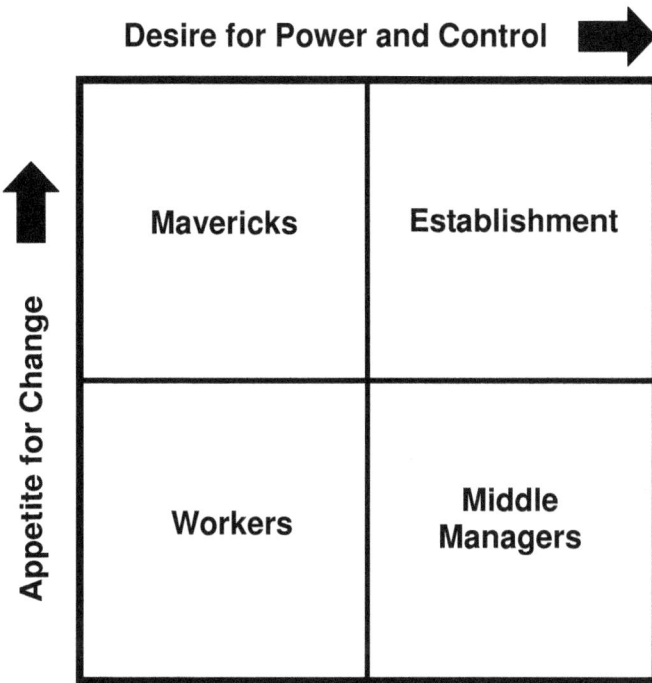

Desire for Power and Control ➡️

	Mavericks	Establishment
	Workers	Middle Managers

(vertical axis) **Appetite for Change** ⬆️

The Workers

The Worker's preference is for the status quo. They have a low appetite for change and a preference for others to make decisions. There are often accusations of "change fatigue" associated with this group. The preference for unconscious behaviour is **dependency** – when they want to avoid undertaking the task, they look for someone to tell them what to do. This leads to poor productivity.

The Establishment

The Establishment's preference is for continuous improvement. They have a high appetite for change and control. There are often accusations of being disengaged from reality associated with this group. They are committed to setting the organisational direction and achieving its desired goals. The preference for unconscious behaviour is **messianic** – when they want to avoid undertaking the task, they are looking for miraculous intervention. This leads to inability to give appropriate direction, organisational lethargy and the influx of management consultants.

The Middle Managers

The Middle Manager's preference is for containment. They have a low appetite for change but a high desire for control. There are often accusations of "micro-management" and "the inability to delegate" associated with this group. They are committed to their colleagues and are interdependent. The preference for unconscious behaviour is fight/flight – when they want to avoid undertaking the task, they either actively argue or passively avoid doing it – with the preference for **flight** (as this passive approach does not draw the ire of the Establishment). The desire to be in control can lead to anxiety, the creation of silos and subsequent resistance and/or inability to change.

The Mavericks

The Maverick's preference is critique. They have a high appetite for change, but a low desire to be in control. There are often accusations that they are "not part of the team". They are highly independent and committed to the outcomes of the organisation. Their preference for unconscious behaviour is fight/flight – when they want to avoid undertaking the task, they either actively argue or passively avoid doing it – with the preference for **fight**. Their critical nature can lead to isolation and disenfranchisement.

A Paradigm Shift

There is another way look at the model, away from the traditional organisational structure, which arranges these four groups independently. Rather than placing people within the organisation into these groups, people can be considered as taking on parts of the functions required by each group. The groups can be considered as interlocking circles:

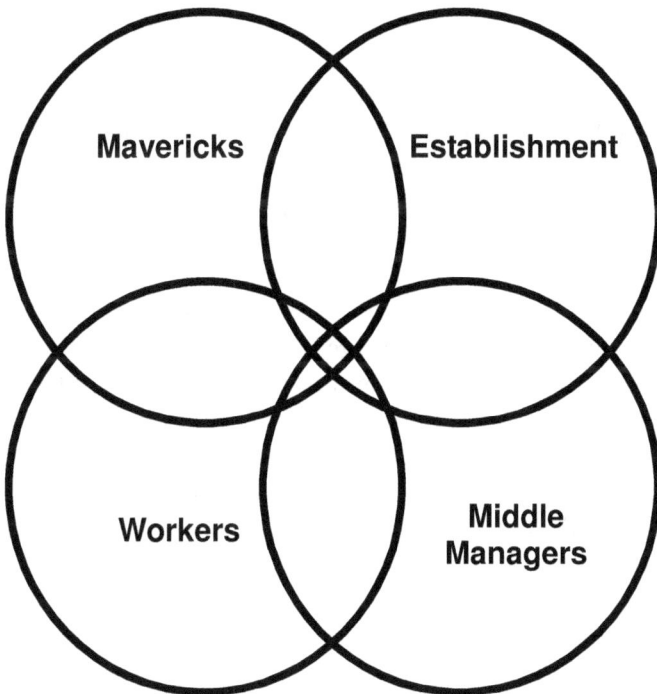

Individuals can be placed anywhere on the diagram, but the most productive place is towards the centre. It is best to look at the overlaps.

As Workers take on responsibility for the outcome of the organisation, they can also manage the boundaries and resources required (the Middle Manager's' role). As they seek to improve the way the organisation achieves its outcomes, they can initiate change and innovation (the Maverick's role). As they are empowered to do these things, they have the opportunity to take on the ability to affect the direction of the organisation (the Establishment's role).

The diagram also illustrates where the most potential for conflict exists. This is where the least overlap occurs; between the Establishment and the Workers, and between the Middle Managers and the Mavericks. The conflict between the Establishment and the Workers is a time-honoured tradition and has been analysed in depth for centuries. However, less is understood about the interaction between Middle Managers and Mavericks.

The tension between the Middle Managers and the Mavericks revolves around the management of boundaries. Intuitively, the Middle Managers aim to tighten their boundaries and "run interference" on external influences that are perceived to affect the performance of the team. This is how "silos" are often created. Mavericks tend to do the opposite. They do not accept the status quo and challenge the effectiveness of the boundaries.

The art of a successful Establishment is its ability to manage the tension between the Mavericks and the Middle Managers without destroying the emotional containment required for the Workers to successfully deliver the organisational outcomes.

While this type of theory is often espoused by post-modernists and the "self-managed" organisational school of thought, the reality is that different people are comfortable in different zones of the diagram; however, this can change over time. Organisations with the flexibility to allow individuals and teams to operate in the zone that best suit their emotional needs will tend to get the best outcomes. It is also important to remember that the reason for the existence of Middle Managers is to maintain a level of practicality in the number of relationships that need to be managed.

The danger is to underestimate the value and importance of having the "requisite variety" to enable each zone to blossom. "Requisite variety" maintains that the internal diversity of any self-regulating system must match the variety and complexity of its environment to deal with the challenges posted by that environment. In other words, trying to manage complex organisations within complex operating environments using simplistic management systems is bound to fail. The ability to look at how organisations undertake their tasks from different perspectives and synthesize these into a coherent operating environment makes the potential for innovation and awesome outcomes possible.

This requires not only a diversity of opinion and thought, but also a bounded structure to contain the anxiety that comes from the confluence of different opinions. The Establishment are still required to decide on the direction of the organisation. However, they ignore their Mavericks, Middle Managers and Workers at their own peril. Under-bounded organisations are not good at giving direction;

overbounded organisations give too much direction. The art is in finding the balance, which can depend on the organisational starting point.

Theorising with Moses

To show how some of this works, it might help to look at the biblical story surrounding Moses.

The ancient Egyptian civilisation can be viewed as a massive organisation that created some awesome outcomes (they were the ones that built the Great Pyramids after all!) The Pharaoh was the Egyptian ruler, with an extensive civil service to run the organisation – these represent the Establishment. The Workers were mostly slaves, which consisted of conquered peoples from surrounding nations, including the nomads of Canaan, the descendants of Jacob who later changed his name to Israel.

The organisation had a substantial Middle Management to improve the productivity of the workers. This often involved lots of yelling and the use of whips.

It came to pass that, following an attempt by the Establishment to do some selective population reduction, one of the slave's children ended being brought up in Pharaoh's household. His name was Moses.

Being brought up in Pharaoh's household, he had a good understanding of the Establishment, but was also made aware of his Worker heritage from his mother who had cared for him as a child.

As a young man, he noticed one of the Middle Managers beating one of the Workers (probably the latest form of behavioural management employed by the Establishment to improve performance). Thinking that this was not such a good idea, he decided to intervene and do away with the Middle Manager. This is a common Maverick mistake – seeking to do away with Middle Managers because they can't see the wood for the trees.

As can be expected, he was persecuted by the Middle Management, and the Establishment tried to do away with him for not being a "team player". So he ran away for a few years.

After a bit of divine coaxing, Moses went back to Pharaoh and suggested that it might be a good idea to allow the Workers a bit of time off to deal with some of their personal and spiritual needs. This was not seen as a productive measure by the Establishment, so a new campaign was started to increase productivity. The Middle Managers were instructed to alter the work practices so that not only were the Workers to make bricks, they also had to gather the raw materials. However, they still had to produce the same number of bricks.

Hence began the well-rehearsed argument between the Establishment and the Workers involving the perception of laziness and unreasonable demands. The Middle Managers, now caught in the all-too-familiar Middle Management squeeze, were at a loss to know how to resolve the situation.

Seeing that things had gone from bad to worse, the Workers now turned on Moses and blamed him for the predicament. Moses replied to the Workers that a new innovative scheme was being hatched involving divine intervention, but they did not believe him. They could not see beyond the hardship of their current work practices to believe that there were better things coming.

Moses needed to approach the Establishment and gain some credibility in order to alter the outcome for the Workers. The Establishment were a bit slow to come to terms with this, but that is for another chapter!

13 Transitions

An important concept for the implementation of innovation and the management of change is transitions and the management of space. As part of my management development at the water authority, I was invited to be part an executive development program. It involved a number of people from different parts of the organisation and was facilitated by a management consultant, who was also an organisational grief counsellor.

It was a privilege to be involved with this group and the facilitator was excellent. It was the involvement with this group that led me to undertake further study in organisational development years later.

The facilitator had devised a process for assisting organisations with managing very difficult change and one of the key concepts was:

$$\text{Change} = \text{Loss} + \text{Gain}$$

Whenever we implement innovation or changes in an organisation, something is lost and something is gained. We leave behind the old and hopefully take on something better and new. A key part in making the change succeed is to recognise and mourn the loss and allow it to pass – much like we do at the death of a loved one; we lament that they are gone and celebrate the life that they had, but we move on.

If we do not move on, the consequences can be catastrophic. There is the example of an engineering company that was struggling with the change in technologies from the slide-rule to computers. Expertise with the slide-rule had become a symbol of competency within the company, and there was a great reluctance to use calculators and computers. The company went from being an industry leader to gradually declining and was eventually taken over by another company.

There was a similar situation at the engineering consultancy I first worked with in moving from pen and ink drawings to computer-aided drafting. The company was very reluctant to invest in the new technology. It took the maverick efforts of the chief draftsperson, and many unpaid hours of work, to develop a system that worked so the company would take up the technology. They eventually did, and are still a very successful engineering consultancy. The art of drafting was a great loss. Gone are the days of the draftsperson using a scalpel to meticulously cut up plastic film they had spent days drawing on when the stupid engineer (that's me) decides that it wasn't needed any more!

Creating Transitional Space

In order to transition from one way of working to another, the concept of allowing space for the transition to occur is important. The space consists of the physical, the emotional and the unconscious. The first two are relatively easy to manage, the third is more difficult, but can be the most damaging if mismanaged or overlooked.

As an example of creating transitional space, we undertake simulation exercises for incident management training. We come up with a simulated disaster scenario for the organisation to manage. They are very intense exercises, both for the participants and the event managers. At the end of the exercise we deliberately provide space for the participants to transition back to "normal life".

Firstly, we make them leave the room in which the exercise was undertaken. We give them a short break and then require them to return to the room. In some instances, we will take them on a walk around the building. While they are gone, we rearrange the room and set it up for a debriefing. We manage the physical space – the room in which the incident occurs no longer exists and the room has returned to normal.

Secondly, when they re-enter the room, we have an informal meal, normally lunch, but sometimes dinner. We encourage the participants to chat amongst themselves about how the exercise went. We are careful to note if anyone is particularly distressed and we might take them aside for an "emotional" debrief. This is very rarely required. We use this forum for the participants to manage their own emotional space. It is extremely inappropriate to allow staff to vent their emotional concerns in a formal, organisational setting where senior management are present. This is not a "normal" work situation. Senior managers often misunderstand the participants' responses, which can affect their career development.

Simulation exercises can be poor indicators of how people behave in normal life. The structure of the simulation exercise will affect the way individuals behave. They are constructed with controlled boundaries to elicit certain types of behaviours related to the role being undertaken by the individual. That is, the outcome is a manipulated one. The results can be quite devastating, as was shown in the Stanford prison experiment. This experiment involved the simulation of a prison environment using university students. The students were placed into two groups randomly – guards and prisoners. The results were that the students took on the roles to such a dramatic and violent extent that the experiment had to be abandoned.

Thirdly, we have a formal debrief of the exercise. We discuss the things that went well, and the things that could have been done better, and produce an action plan for improvement to the organisation. The participants are given time to fill out a questionnaire on how they felt the exercise was run, not on the exercise itself. Then we close the exercise, seeking to tie off the boundary of the exercise, with the aim of managing the unconscious space. It is very important for the participants to leave the exercise and come back to "normal" life.

Occasionally, some people do not come back for the debrief. This has sometimes affected their performance in the workplace over the next few weeks. In one case a senior manager could not return for the debrief, and had difficulties relating to his staff over the following weeks. He had a number of concerns regarding some of the things that happened during the exercise, but others did not seem to have the same degree of concern. The staff had reconciled the difficulties and saw a way forward, whereas the senior manager had not done this. Fortunately, we were able to spend a few hours debriefing the exercise with him and the workplace returned to its usual hectic chaos.

So allowing space and time for people to work through change is extremely important.

The Confusion Room

Another point of transition is the confusion room. People need time and space to assimilate new ides within their current world perspective, and this can create confusion within a group – particularly if the group is trying to plan a way forward in an organisation. This is a normal part of any planning process, and essential if each member of the group is going to accept the outcomes of the process.

I once assisted the directors and executive of a retail organisation with their annual strategic review. The morning session had been quite hectic. While there had been much discussion, there were very few outcomes. I had the presence of mind to realise that the group was in the confusion room and the break for lunch was going to be very important. During the lunch break the Chairman took me aside and made known his concerns that very little seemed to have been achieved in the morning session. I explained to him the concept of the confusion room and asked him to trust me that everything would come together in the afternoon session.

At this point the Chairman, like so many leaders of the Establishment in this situation, had to make a decision to continue or to intervene. I had faith that the group would achieve the desired outcomes by the end of the day. They were all highly intelligent and successful business people, they just needed to be operating on the same page. So often leaders in this situation lose faith in their colleagues' abilities and take control of the situation. They tend to force outcomes that can often be at times inappropriate and also lose the full support of the group.

Fortunately, I had assisted the Chairman in the past with some cultural change process at another organisation and he had enough faith to let me continue with the strategic planning process. The day ended up with a very clear direction for the business, including a number of tasks to be undertaken by the executive to determine how the direction was to be achieved.

The confusion room is a necessary part of transition. It is important to guide people through the room and provide space and time for them to understand their surroundings, rather than drag them out the nearest convenient exit. It is also important not to let people get stuck in the confusion room. Keeping people stuck in the confusion room can have some long-lasting, detrimental effects on organisational performance.

Reverse Culture Shock
During my University years, I visited Papua New Guinea and worked in the engineering department of a mission base that accommodated about a thousand people from many nationalities. Papua New Guinea is a culturally diverse and politically clan based nation. The clan allegiance and identity is much stronger than the national identity. While it is a relatively poor country, the clan structure ensures that people are generally well looked after and there is little destitution.

It was my first experience away from home, and I had to deal with the cultural differences between my culture and the Papua New Guineans, as well as the differences between my culture and that of Europeans and North Americans. I had expected to have to adapt to living among the Papua New Guinean culture but I was unprepared for the effect of the differences between my culture and the North Americans. It took me quite a long time to adjust.

This phenomenon is often called culture shock. It is the disorientation we feel when we are outside our own comfort zone and are required to adapt to another way of working or thinking. Our perspective of the world is often deeply challenged. Sometimes we embrace the challenge and our world view is enhanced. Sometimes we are repelled and retreat into a smaller self-contained world where home-sickness and a reluctance to relate to the new environment is all consuming.

Having to adjust my view of the world gave me a greater appreciation for where I had come from, which was probably my way of coping with home-sickness. I had left home with ambivalence regarding my own culture and returned with a great deal more respect and a feeling of comfort.

However, when I returned home, I felt even more disorientated. My experience had a dramatic effect on my view of the world, but I found this very difficult to explain to my family and friends. They were genuinely interested in my experience, but I couldn't seem to communicate this effectively. The main reason for this is that while I had been through an experience that had affected my own thinking and emotional processes, my family and friends had not had an equivalent experience. This phenomenon is often called reverse culture shock.

Reverse culture shock is often experienced in organisations when people go away to undertake external training, or even work in a different department, and then return and find it difficult to settle back in. It is very important to provide an opportunity for them to be debriefed and verbalise their experience.

Here are a few suggestions for implementing innovation and change:

- Recognise and release things that are lost.
- Allow space for the transition - physical, emotional and unconscious.
- Be comfortable with the confusion room.
- Make sure the confusion room is only temporary.
- Embrace the new.
- Recognise changes in others.
- Debrief those who experience the wider world through temporary dislocation.

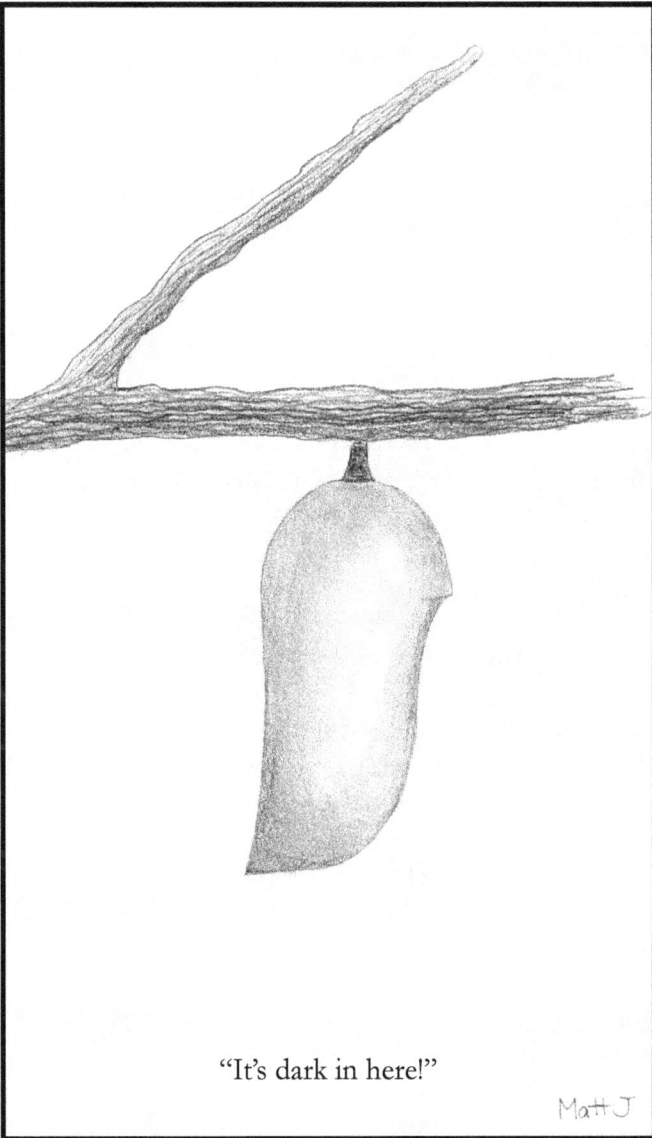

"It's dark in here!"

Matt J

14   The Shadow Organisation

"Power tends to corrupt, absolute power corrupts absolutely" - John Acton

All organisations have shadows, especially those that have existed for a long period of time. The water authority has existed, in one form or another, as a bureaucratic institution for over one hundred years. It is older than the country's national parliament. When it was formed, the Board of management consisted of representatives from the local municipalities – 39 members in all. This grew to 54 members by the late 1970's. As can be imagined, getting this many members to agree on strategic direction was always going to be a challenge. This gave significant power to the position of Chairman.

Accumulated Power
The water authority also grew in power and responsibility. It began with managing water and sewerage infrastructure, to eventually being responsible for drains and waterways, main roads, bridges, parks, foreshore management, regulation of buses and taxis, tramways as well as cemeteries and crematoria. Most powerful of all, it became responsible for town planning. Very little could be built in the city without its approval.

The authority had the power to set its own revenue collection and had wide ranging legislative authority. Local government and the community often saw it as a law unto itself. In an effort to dilute the power of the authority, the local government bodies convinced the state government to hold an inquiry into the operations and practices of the authority. Ironically, the main recommendation of the inquiry was to removal local government representation from the water authority's Board of management.

Government Intervention

As often happens with powerful bureaucracies, the power base starts to encroach on the government's own power base. Governments often struggle to accept power sharing and soon step in to rectify the situation. During the 1980's the government lost faith in the authority and by the early 1990's had removed all the planning and auxiliary functions; returning the authorities' responsibilities solely to water, sewerage and stormwater.

Together with the loss of planning and the ability to control the external environment, the authority increasingly found itself tied to new rules from the environmental regulator and more intrusive and powerful government departments. As such, it turned its need for control internally. Through the mid-1980's to the mid-1990's there were massive industrial disputes and continuous restructuring. At one point there was a general strike by the operations staff, which resulted in lock-outs at the treatment plants requiring management to undertake the operational responsibilities.

Destabilisation

The stability of the authority started to dissipate. The increasing drive to cut costs and reduce staff was followed by serious asset degradation and infrastructure failure. The spilling of millions of litres of raw sewage into rivers and the closing of bayside beaches caused the authority to lose much credibility within the community. It was no longer seen as a protector of the environment, but as a poor manager of community resources.

Whole sections of the organisation were contracted out during this period. The water authority's internal management of these contractors was generally poor. Costs escalated, service provision declined and the relationship between the staff and the contractors was abysmal. Very few of the service contracts were renewed when they expired.

Organisational Shadow

I joined the water authority soon after this period of significant change. I had started in the regional office, which had been newly created and had quite a positive social atmosphere attached to it. However, the head office was a depressing place. Staff generally kept to themselves, didn't take annual leave in case they were retrenched and were just plain sad. This was more noticeable in those staff that had been with the water authority for a long time.

One Managing Director, who came from outside the water industry, attempted to devolve power into the organisation but did not recognise the underbounded nature of the authority, which hindered the ability to achieve effective outcomes. What I have not spoken about is the autocratic organisational shadow that had been infused over many decades.

◆ ◆ ◆

To understand the Jungian concept of a shadow, some understanding of psychodynamics is required.

Organisations are made up of people and as such can reflect both the conscious and unconscious patterns of behaviour of those people. Two things that affect people's behaviour are uncertainty and anxiety (although one can lead to the other).

Freudian/Klienian psychology contends that people operate on an emotional spectrum from depressive to paranoid/schizoid. The depressive is the normal, well balanced mode of operation, where actions are mainly controlled by conscious thought. The paranoid/schizoid is an unbalanced mode of operation, where actions are mainly controlled by unconscious thought.

During our daily lives we tend to waver between both perspectives, depending on the circumstance, the anxiety we encounter and our emotional ability to manage this anxiety. When we operate in the depressive state, we tend to see others as whole people, with good and bad attributes. When we operate in the paranoid/schizoid, we tend to see people as either all good or all bad. This is often called splitting, where the good or bad attributes are emphasised, while the counter is repressed. When we split, we project our good or bad feeling onto the person (commonly called "dumping"). If they take on the feelings and identify with our projections, we temporarily feel better. This is called projective identification.

How does this work in an organisation? Your boss chastises you for a poor report that you have submitted. This makes you feel anxious, but also a bit guilty that you could have done a better job. This creates the emotional state of feeling helpless. You meet one of your staff as you walk back to your office. Some menial issue springs to mind and you think that this person is "always" making mistakes. You "dump" on them about the issue and transfer your feeling of helplessness. They go away feeling sad and helpless. You suddenly feel pretty good having "lost" the sense of helplessness.

When they confront you about the incident some time later in the day you hardly remember that it happened. By the end of the day you are extremely tired and can feel a migraine starting. While you have unconsciously transferred your anxiety onto the unsuspecting staff member, the emotional energy required to maintain the position is substantial, hence the tiredness.

Organisations are made up of people interacting with each other so this process continues day in, day out. The more anxiety and uncertainty that is created within the organisation, the more people create defensive mechanisms to survive the emotional barrage. When they collude on the defensive mechanism, it becomes a social defence system – an unconscious social norm. An organisational shadow develops that affects the behaviour of people in the organisation; behaviour which can seem illogical and out of character. It often affects the types of groups that form and the way people are promoted.

Defensive mechanisms can further develop into shadows that affect whole industries or sectors. These are referred to as social defence fabrics. This can become evident in institutions and professions that have been around for generations. They include utilities such as power and water, medical and educational institutions and the finance sector. Failures, such as the global financial crisis, can be looked at through the social defence fabric in place that hindered appropriate governance and effective risk management.

As an example of this, there is an apocryphal story of a large accounting/management consulting company during the global financial crisis. They had developed a way of approaching their work that was effective but also created a homogenous clan-type culture. Promotion became linked to the understanding and successful implementation of the way of working within the organisation. The company became very successful. However, their method of managing their work also became a unconscious way in which uncertainty and anxiety was managed in the organisation – a shadow culture had started to form.

The senior partners (the Establishment) were sufficiently aware and came to understand that the culture had become too homogenous. Some diversity was required to ensure that it survived the challenges of a changing external environment (requisite variety). To deal with this, they sought to replace a percentage of staff at each level of the organisation with outside professionals. This created significant anxiety in the organisation, and, rather than transforming the existing culture, the existing shadow culture was reinforced. People within the organisation unconsciously colluded to make it very difficult for the new staff. Within twelve months most of the new staff had left the organisation. Not long after the global financial crisis appeared, and since their way of undertaking work did not have a mechanism to cope, the company collapsed.

It is difficult to even observe the shadow, much less manage it, because most of the processing is done in our unconscious thought. The most appropriate way to manage this phenomenon is to seek to operate as much as possible from the depressive rather than the paranoid-schizoid position. It is very closely linked to the discussion earlier on bounded organisations. While stress and anxiety are a normal part of our everyday lives, successful organisations are able to contain the anxiety and create productive rather than pathological outlets for its expression. The more the emotional response to these stresses is repressed, the more likely the organisation will create an unconscious shadow and a culture that is epitomised by "silos" and scapegoating.

These shadows tend to push organisations to manage risk poorly, both overcompensating for perceived risks, creating economic inefficiencies, and being unprepared for external and structural risks. This leads to business instability.

I do not profess to be an expert in recognising organisational shadows, but here are a few suggestions:

- Determine the unwritten rules in an organisation and try to find patterns that link to operational procedures which are counter-productive.
- Watch how people react in stressful situations. This is when the shadows appear. Look for patterns of behaviour and try to link these to the causes of anxiety, not the anxiety itself or the behaviour. Treat the behaviour as a symptom, not a cause.
- Bring in external people to observe meetings and reflect back on the processes used at the end of the meeting. Be careful, these people should not be involved in the meeting, or have a stake in the outcome. The shadow will affect them as well.
- Focus on organisational outcomes. Watch where the divergence occurs and seek to determine the cause of the divergence.

Awesome Outcome Principle:

Understanding organisational shadows can remove potential barriers to creating awesome outcomes.

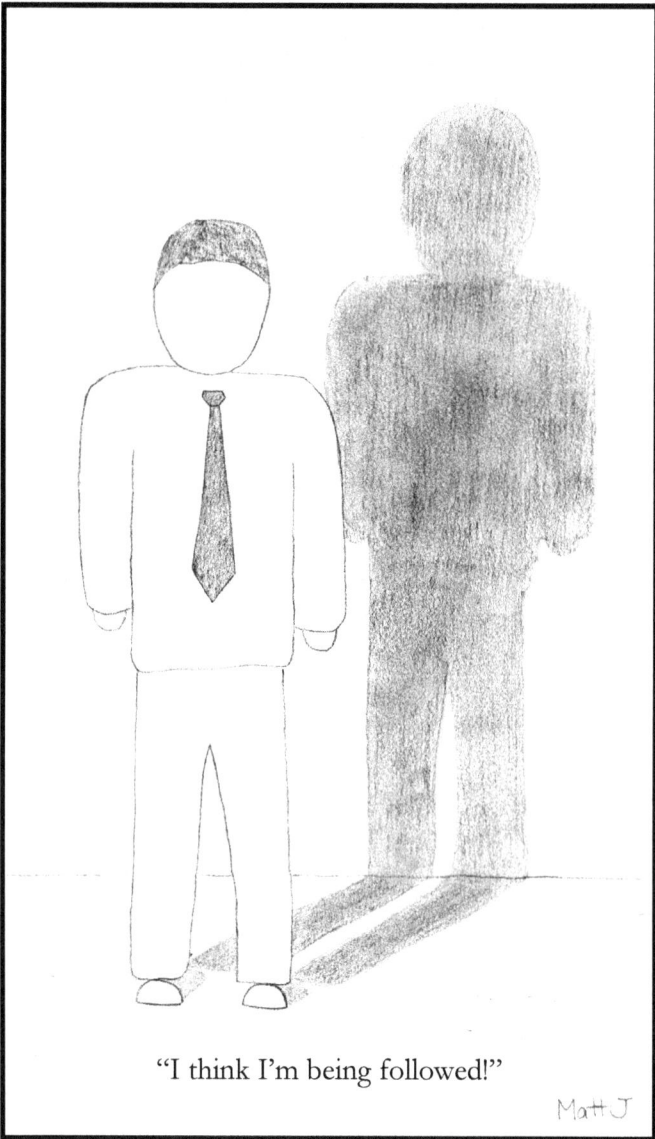

"I think I'm being followed!"

Matt J

Post Script

I had come into the water authority with youthful enthusiasm and energy. However, I observed a distinctive air of fatigue among many of the middle managers who had long careers with the water authority. A senior manager commented in a meeting one day that he was sick and tired of corporate restructuring, and having to tell people they no longer had a job.

I had the feeling that the domination of employees had become the organisational shadow, and this was taking its toll throughout the organisation, which even the external Managing Director could not overcome. He finally succumbed and left the organisation. His replacement was a long time water authority employee well accustomed to the organisational shadow.

15   Pathological Establishment

"Analysis does not set out to make pathological reactions impossible, but to give the patient's ego freedom to decide one way or another." - Sigmund Freud

My country is the oldest, lowest, flattest and driest continental land mass apart from the Antarctic. The "outback" is a vast, arid area of the country which has minimal habitable land. It covers over two-thirds of the county. The majority of the population is concentrated down the eastern coastline.

It is also a land of extremes. Years of drought can be followed by horrendous floods. Very few people take water for granted and the long term planning of water supplies for major cities is essential.

Water Supply Planning
Drinking water supplies can be collected from a number of sources; surface water stored in reservoirs, ground water, treated water from wastewater treatment plants and desalinated water from the oceans.

The majority of our drinking water comes from surface water stored in reservoirs. To determine whether the water storages are adequate, hydrologists look at the historical rainfall patterns and use stochastic (times series) modelling to determine whether the future water demand for cities can be met from the existing resources. This has become more complicated in recent years, as the historical rainfall patterns are required to be amended to reflect the potential effects of climate variation (whether human-induced or natural).

Water Security

It is not generally cost effective to provide water resources for large cities that ensure water demand can be met all of the time. Governments use the concept of demand management by restricting the use of water in very dry rainfall years – what is usually called a drought. People are restricted on the amount of water they can use on their gardens, to wash their cars and so on. Water security is the term used to discuss how often people may be restricted in water usage. This can be described as a recurrence interval – once in ten years or as a statistical percentage – 90% which is close to once in ten years, 95% is close to once in twenty years and 99% is close to once in a hundred years. The cost for increasing the percentage of security is exponential, and the normal range that is economical is between 90 and 95%.

It is not really possible to have 100% water security, no matter what people desire. There is always the potential for something to go wrong. The longer there is unrestricted demand, the more people take their water supplies for granted, the more water they use and the more additional resources are required to maintain the supply.

One of the difficulties undertaking effective water supply planning is that the planning needs to be ten to twenty years ahead of need to build cost effective infrastructure. The political cycle is only three to four years and unless the water authorities are courageous enough to challenge short-sighted political whims, the planning process can be distorted with consequential poor and costly investment decisions.

The Millennium Drought

The 1990s had been a period of above average rainfall and the water reservoirs that fed the city were over 80% full. Rather than continuing to fill the reservoirs, a decision was made to run the excess water through a small hydro-electric power plant to gain some inconsequential revenue. There were a number of years of water in these reservoirs, so maintenance was reduced on infrastructure relater to two other water sources, making one unusable and reducing the capacity of the other.

The next potential major water source was politically sensitive, so the long term plan was to only use the existing resources and manage demand using customer self-regulation (demand management). No effective long-term planning was undertaken to develop possible future additional major water sources. Murphy's law intervened, and thus began the driest period of rainfall on record exacerbated by the spectre of climate change with its implications of reduced reliability of surface water and its negative effect on reservoir storage levels. Planning to undertake new water resources takes time for efficient implementation. The government panicked, took the control of the implementation of the next water resource away from the water authority and implemented their own solution through a government department at an enormous cost to the community. It was clear that something needed to be done, but the under-bounded nature of the authority made it unprepared for the crisis.

Behavioural management

Prior to the drought the water authority had successfully removed the Managing Director who had come from private industry, and had decided to install a new Managing Director from "the good old days". This resulted in a significant change in the executive team, and the eventual restructuring of the organisation back to the functional divisions approach.

The executive sought to implement a set of "core values" to manage staff behaviour in an attempt to improve productivity. They were to be the values that employees should espouse and the behaviours that should be modelled.

A draft form of the core values was circulated to staff for comment. However, when the final core values were released, the only change was to remove the words "behaviours we aspire to" from the introduction. So the core values were decreed:

- Innovation (Not being content with the status quo; having the courage to seek a better way).
- Enthusiasm (Having a positive attitude and enjoying work).
- Co-operation (Being a team player. Sharing knowledge and supporting each other to benefit our customers, community and our business).
- Pride (Doing your best. Portraying our organisation and yourself in a positive way. Having a professional approach to work).
- Respect (Caring about our fellow employees, our customers and the community. Honouring commitments).

- Integrity (Understanding and abiding by the code of conduct).

I struggled with the notion that these were all values. I had no problems with Respect and Integrity. In my business today, these are two of the values my own staff have identified as important (although integrity is not linked to any code of conduct). Our third one is honesty, which does not appear in the above list. Our fourth is "being financially sound".

Innovation is a means to an end – not the goal itself. Being innovative can create awesome outcomes, but it can also be inappropriate when tried and tested means of achieving an outcome is more effective and economical.

Enthusiasm, Co-operation and Pride are all double-edged swords. They are subjective, and are more often than not used as manipulative tools. How often has a manager or a colleague used the term "not a team player" when they do not want to listen to alternative approaches or want individuals to undertake a task that borders on being unethical? Sometimes work is hard and not enjoyable. To be criticised for not being "enthusiastic" when it is really hard to even be there is not helpful. Being unrealistically positive is not effective in developing a long-term viable organisation. When critical evaluation is undermined because "only positive attitudes" are valued, organisations fail, often catastrophically. One only needs to look at the failure of the global financial sector during the first decade of this millennium, where the unrealistic positive view that the stock market would continue to rise became unstuck, and many companies no longer exist.

The core values were presented to the Middle Managers and the Workers on a "take it or leave it basis". The unambiguous message directed at the Workers was that they were expected to unquestioningly promote and adhere to the core values or leave the organisation.

There was an instance where one of the work teams made some light-hearted fun of the "core values". This found its way back to the personnel department, where the wrath of the executive was manifest. People were accused of disloyalty. Managers were told to control their staff. Senior managers were summoned to the Managing Directors office to "please explain". People very nearly lost their jobs over the incident.

◆ ◆ ◆

While the example may seem trivial, the vehemency of the executive's response would make a Spanish Inquisitor blush. The rightness or wrongness of the employees' response is not the issue at stake. The disproportional response to the offences by the executive borders on the pathological and hints at more deeply underlying issues within the organisation.

While core values may be seen as behavioural traits to aspire to, the potential for harm to occur to both individuals and the organisation in the guise of upholding the core values is ever present in a hierarchical organisation.

The overemphasis on the control of behaviour as a means to improve organisational performance is risky because it is nearly impossible to predict the long term consequences, particularly on the psychological and emotional make-up of the employees. One of the consequences of the executives' response above was the creation of an organisation that was unwilling to critically review its actions, and those of its owners (the government), therefore it was not able to provide credible advice on future asset investment. This was the backdrop to the failure of the water authority to manage its water resources discussed above.

Well-investigated and documented examples of pathological failures are the Challenger and Columbia space shuttle incidents at NASA.

On January 28, 1986 the Challenger space shuttle "exploded" on take-off due to the failure of "O-ring" seals in the booster rockets. The spacecraft was destroyed and seven lives were lost. As a consequence the shuttle fleet was grounded for three years.

On February 1, 2003 the Columbia space shuttle disintegrated on re-entry as a result of damage to heat shield tiles during lift-off. The spacecraft was destroyed and seven lives were lost. As a consequence the shuttle fleet was grounded for two years.

The findings from the Columbia Investigations Board included a number of institutional issues that resulted in the failure of the Columbia space shuttle:

- Reliance on past success as a substitute for sound engineering practices.
- Organisational barriers that prevented effective communication of critical safety measures and stifled differences of opinions.
- Lack of integrated management across program areas.

- Informal chain of command and decision making process that operated outside the organisational rules.

Even more telling is that these findings are very similar to the issues surrounding the failure of the Challenger space shuttle seventeen years earlier. Dr Diane Vaughan, who had undertaken a sociological investigation of the Challenger incident, is quoted during the Columbia investigation as saying "What we find out from a comparison between Columbia and Challenger is that NASA as an organisation did not learn from its previous mistakes and it did not properly address all of the factors that the [Challenger] presidential commission identified".

It is evident that the shadow culture within NASA was pervasive – even though there had been seventeen years of cultural change and behavioural modification programs, the underlying causes of the organisational failures had not been adequately addressed, with disastrous consequences.

Pharaoh, Freud and Free Will

Earlier, I used the biblical story of Moses and the Egyptian Pharaoh to illustrate the interaction between the Establishment, Mavericks, Middle Managers and Workers. The conclusion of the story illustrates how I think a pathological organisation (or individual) is created.

My starting position is that we all have choices, and the choices we make, either actively or passively, have the potential to limit future choices.

Moses wanted the Pharaoh to treat the Workers better, and when the Establishment made a choice to make life harder for them, the stakes were increased. With a bit of divine help, plagues of blood and frogs swept the land of Egypt. Now the inner circle of the Establishment (wise men and magicians) was also able to duplicate these plagues, so Pharaoh decided to ignore Moses pleas and "hardened his heart".

After a few more plagues (gnats, flies and dead livestock), which the inner circle could not duplicate, the Establishment started to become concerned. However, Pharaoh was convinced he was in the right and the inner circle refused to disagree. Pharaoh continued to ignore Moses' pleas and "hardened his heart".

The plagues became more serious (boils, hail, locusts and darkness), but there was a change in Pharaoh's ability to make choices. No longer did Pharaoh "harden his heart", but "God hardened Pharaoh's heart". Putting aside the theological difficulties with this phrase, the analogy to a Freudian defence mechanism is apparent. Pharaoh could no longer make a rational decision, but was "programmed" by the previous poor decisions that he had made.

Finally when the last plague, the death of the first born, pervaded Egypt, Pharaoh acquiesced to Moses' plea. But even then, Pharaoh reneged, and pursued Moses, only to be drowned in the sea.

As organisations continue to make poor decisions, it can become increasingly difficult to stop making them. The behavioural control sought by the Establishment is often directed at supporting the unconscious decision making process. They become pathological. It becomes nearly impossible to create real cultural change, and the ability to innovate is stifled.

Rather than trying to control behaviour, here are a few suggestions for managing good organisational outcomes:

- Set clear objectives.
- Focus on achieving the objectives.
- Do not interfere too much with the day to day operation of groups.
- Have good governance arrangements and feedback mechanisms to manage deviations from the outcome required.
- Spend significant resources on developing senior managers' ability to manage outcomes rather than behaviour.
- Get external intervention if the culture has become pathological.

Awesome Outcome Principle:

Seeking to control behaviour tends to stifle awesome outcomes.

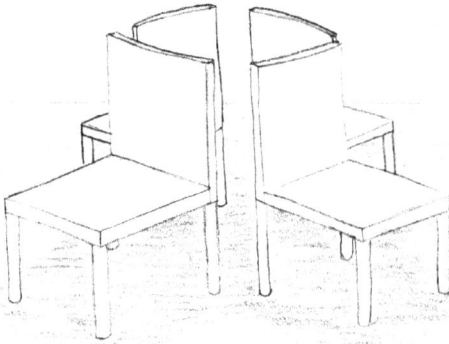

Management recruitment process.

Post Script.

It is an eerie co-incidence that the failure of the sewerage system and the failure to plan the water supply system had a similar intervening time frame as the failure of the two space shuttles. As with NASA, the water authority had undergone significant cultural change programs and behavioural management between incidents, but the underlying pathological culture remained. Most noticeably, the Mavericks had been effectively silenced.

It was just prior to the failure to plan the water supply system that I decided to leave the organisation. A more senior position had opened up within the water authority, and for a number of reasons I was reluctant to apply for it. However, the divisional manager strongly urged me to apply, so I did. The interview did not go well, much of it revolving around expected executive management behaviour and obedience. As one of my managers had once said to me years before, I was great at my job, but not so good at massaging the egos of the executive. He meant it as a criticism; I took it as a compliment.

16   Managing Silos

"Communication is not a matter of being right, but of starting a flow of energy between two people that can result in mutual understanding – John Sanford.

When I started at the water authority, it was structured along functional lines. The planning engineers, accountants and human resources personnel were located in head office in the centre of the city. The maintenance and operational personnel were located at major facilities, such as dams, water treatment plants and sewage treatment plants.

Working at Head Office

Head office was a multi-storey building, laid out strictly by function. The accountants were on one floor, the water planning engineers another, the sewage planning engineers yet another, and at the top were the executive and strategic planners.

At the major facilities, the operators would often have a control room with small offices attached, while the maintenance personnel were often in a separate building. It was colour coded as well – the operators wore white overalls and the maintenance staff wore blue overalls.

The authority had been through major restructuring in the years before I joined. Many staff had been retrenched, and sadly much of the human side had been inappropriately managed. There were people who had spent their lives undertaking repetitive tasks, such as mowing grass at reservoirs, only for the work to be outsourced because it was perceived to be more efficient. When I joined I had to take a medical examination with the water authority's doctor. She quipped that she was out of practice inducting new people; she had only been dealing with outgoing employees!

Not surprisingly, the authority suffered from poor communication and a self-preservation culture. In my first year I only met a finance person once. The authority had dual management streams – engineering and finance. To get an approval for a project from the Board, it had to be approved and signed off at every level in both management streams. This could take months. Often a sentence would be changed at one level and reversed at the next level. Through a series of events both my immediate manager and the section manager were seconded to do other things. I ended up acting manager of the section and decided to flex my newly inherited powers.

Project Approval

The approval process began with a draft requisition being placed on a file with supporting documentation. The file was then sent on a cascading journey from finance to engineering at each level of the management hierarchy. In the engineering stream we were tired of the petty corrections that would come back from every level of the finance stream. This was part of the self-preservation culture. It was sometimes felt that if a change was not made to the requisition, does that reviewer really need to exist? It's a bit like the philosophical debate around if a tree falls in the forest, and no-one is around to hear it, does it make a sound?

When a correction was required, we would get the requisition retyped, remove the original draft from the file with its associated comments and send the new draft back again until it was approved. On one occasion, we did not remove the draft copies with the multitude of petty comments attached. We left the marked up requisition on file and added the new revised requisition. Eventually the file had over a dozen corrected requisitions attached before it was to go to the chief finance officer. This process had taken more than four weeks.

This time the file was returned, hand delivered, by a member of the finance division. This was unusual. Normally all documentation went through the internal mail system to reinforce the silo culture of the organisation. I opened the file. All the marked up copies had been removed and the requisition had been approved. With poorly concealed amusement, I thanked the courier and was dourly informed that we needed to improve communication between the divisions.

Planning amongst the Sewage

Following an organisational restructure, I ended up at the large sewage treatment plant. The plant was to be treated as an independent business unit. It employed over a hundred personnel, so a group of finance and human resources people were also moved to the plant along with the planning engineers. The idea was to break the silos and improve communication. I became the planning manager and was responsible for overseeing how the plant was to be upgraded and managing the capital works implementation program.

By "planning", I mean asset planning, not business direction planning. Water authorities are a simple business. Obtain water, treat water, deliver water to customers, take away sewage, treat sewage, dispose or reuse it in a safe, environmentally sensitive manner. While the individual processes may be complex (a modern sewage treatment plant is highly technically complex), the business model is not. Most water authorities are monopolies, so business direction planning really only occurs at the periphery – such as finding markets for recycled water.

I have a fairly simplistic view of the interactions between planning, maintenance and operations. The role of planning to ensure that there is sufficient infrastructure and processes for the operators to meet the intended purpose of the plant and manage the organisational risk. The role of maintenance is to keep the equipment in good operational condition. The intersection between planning and maintenance is asset management – making the most of the equipment and managing refurbishment, replacement and upgrades. This requires good communication between all groups to manage the processes efficiently and effectively.

Working with the Maintenance Team

The maintenance manager introduced me to the team leaders in the maintenance section. All were men with touches of grey in their hair. They were accustomed to speaking their minds and their universal comments revolved around my age and perceived lack of experience. This was quite perceptive. I was young and somewhat naive!

My team worked hard to get the operations and maintenance personnel involved in our work. One project involved radically changing how part of a recycle system worked in the plant. I sent one of the young engineers to discuss the idea with key people around the plant. A week later he came back convinced that it would not work. They wanted the system replaced just how it was. We discussed all the objections, worked out how to solve them and I sent him off to do the rounds again.

We decided to hold a workshop to finalise the solution and invited all the key stakeholders; about twenty people in all. The maintenance manager walked into the room and sidled over to where I was sitting, whispering that I was mad and there was no way this group was going to agree on any-thing. Regardless, we ran the workshop, answered all the concerns and everyone in the room agreed to the project. The maintenance manager was impressed and learned a valuable lesson that day. Never run a workshop without undertaking rigorous investigation and consultation before-hand.

In the past, the planning group and the maintenance group were very effective silos, and communication between them was poor to non-existent. It didn't help that they were sep-arated by thirty kilometres of metropolitan suburbs. Plac-ing the two group within walking distance at the treatment plant made a significant difference to the outcomes achieved.

◆ ◆ ◆

Silo culture is one of the most unhelpful elements in organ-isations for creating awesome outcomes. Innovation and cultural change is stifled by the lack of trust and sharing of information. I once suggested to a senior engineer that it might be helpful if she discussed her solution to a problem with a person in a different section, who I knew was work-ing on a similar problem. I was astounded at the vehe-mence of the negative response. When I asked why she was so opposed, she replied that she didn't want anyone else to steal her idea and get the credit!

Silo culture can also be incredibly difficult to break. In some organisations silo culture is endemic; attempts to break down the communication barriers are met with fierce resistance.

A good way to break down silos is to create multifunctional project teams and change the mix of team members for each project. During my fourth year of university we had a subject called "projects". Over the year we had to complete a number of design projects in teams of three. One of the requirements was that we were not allowed to create teams that had people in them with whom we had already undertaken a previous project. It required us to work with people of different temperaments, skill levels and commitment. It is not surprising that, thirty years later, we are still a very close group of friends.

I have often discussed this process with other engineers. Many of them thought it was unfair to have marks for a subject dependant on working with people that might not be as skilful or committed as they were. It is possible that the individualistic educational system of assessment is where the silo mentality begins. In the "real" world we are required to work with all sorts of people with different skills, temperaments and motivation.

At an organisational level, breaking down silos can be achieved through the use of steering committees and working groups for cross group projects. The steering group consists of representatives of the Establishment and a project manager. The steering group sets the direction and scope of the project and monitor its progress. The project manager's first task is to get agreement on the scope of the project and document the outcomes required. It is an imperative that the project manager is someone who has good communication skills and has the ability to work across functional and/or divisional groups. It doesn't hurt for them to have a bit of Maverick as well.

A working group is established to deliver the project. It is facilitated by the project manager and the group is required to have the appropriate expertise from within and outside the organisation to undertake the project. The project manager is the liaison between the steering group and the working group. It is the project manager's role to keep the steering committee (and hence the Establishment) from interfering with the day-to-day operation of the working group.

To this end the project manager needs the support of the Establishment. As program manager for the capital works program, I had an over-arching responsibility for a huge sewer (four metres diameter) being constructed with a specialised tunnel boring machine. A steering committee had been set up to oversee the project, and it had been operating for a number of years. Unfortunately, there were a number of issues between the project services division and the sewerage division, which were being played out in the steering committee. The steering committee had started to get involved in the day-to-day management of the project – down to critiquing the number of staff managing the project.

The project manager was spending a great deal of time on inappropriate administrative tasks requested by the steering committee. Members of the steering committee were also having their own meetings and making decisions about the project without the knowledge of the project manager. I solved the problem by writing a diplomatic memo to my counterpart in the project services division requesting that all communication at senior levels of the project go through the project manager. This was copied to all of the senior managers in the sewerage group. He replied that he would make sure that this would happen. His reply was copied it to all the senior managers in the project services division. This empowered the project manager to manage the project without undue interference and I was able to get the steering committee to focus on the direction of the project rather than its implementation.

Some suggestions for breaking down silos are:
- Create cross team project groups to encourage people to work together.
- Move staff between groups. I have seen some excellent results from seconding people across functional teams (engineers into human resources and finance, finance people into maintenance teams and so on.) This is very powerful when undertaken with middle managers.
- Have representatives from groups attend other groups' team meetings.
- Break up groups where the silo culture has become endemic. Where the culture is reinforced by senior management, move the senior managers.
- Aim to create an inclusive organisational culture, with clear goals and outcomes.
- Rewards and bonus systems should be heavily weighted on the whole organisational outcome ra-

ther than individual or group performance. The best system that I have worked in was where 25% of performance pay was based on the performance of the whole organisation, 25% was division, 25% was team and 25% was individual.

Awesome Outcome Principle:

Communication and the breaking down of silos are paramount to the creation of awesome outcomes.

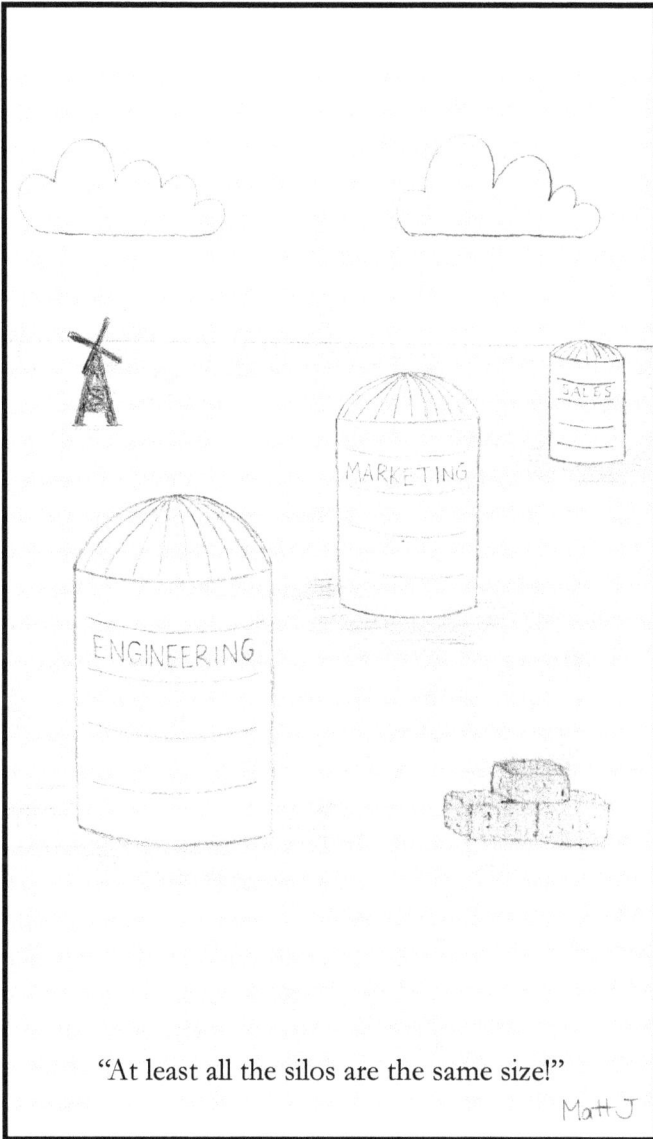

"At least all the silos are the same size!"

Post Script

About a year after I started working at the sewage treatment plant, I was invited to come over and discuss the future of the plant with some of the maintenance personnel. This was part of the practice of improving the information flow between different groups at the plant. Before I started my presentation, one of the group leaders stood up and introduced me with these words: "When Peter first started here we wondered what the organisation had done to us – but now, for the first time in twenty-five years, we all feel a part of the planning process".

While it was probably one of the most difficult years of my working life, my team had worked exceptionally hard to improve the communication of information around the plant. I have undertaken many organisational changes in my working career, but I have never felt so proud of a team and the successful breaking down of an entrenched silo culture.

17   Investigating Failures

"It's fine to celebrate success, but it is important to heed the lessons of failure" – Bill Gates

Following the reassignment of my manager onto a special project, I became responsible for upgrading the capacity of a very large sewage pumping station. The pumping station transferred sewage under a major river in the middle of an affluent residential suburb. If the amount of sewage entering the pumping station exceeded the capacity of the pumps, raw sewage spilt into the river, with the associated colour and odour additions to the environment. This was happening far too often for the sensitivities of the local neighbourhood, so the capacity of the pumping station was to be increased.

All of the major upgrades had been completed. A new pump well, new pumps, pipework and a new switchboard had been installed and were working fine. However, some minor software changes to the control system were required. Pump Number 1 was being renamed Pump Number 2. Pump Number 2 was being renamed Pump Number 1. Nothing very complex – what could go wrong?

In the middle of the night, ten hours after the changes were made, raw sewage was pouring into the waterway from an outlet five kilometres upstream. The problem was rectified reasonably quickly and an incident report was prepared by the project managers, ready and waiting when we arrived at work the next day.

The report was brief. The pump station had a main sewer and a smaller branch sewer connected to it. There was a large penstock (gate) on the branch sewer which could isolate the branch sewer from the pumping station. Closing the penstock would cause sewage to back-up in the branch sewer and eventually spill into the river upstream. These spillage points are called emergency relief structures. They are in all good sewage systems – it is far better and healthier to know where the sewage spills when thing go wrong. It is not so good having it spill into thousands of peoples' homes!

In the control system there were some "soft" registers that operated the status of many of the control valves – including the penstock. When control system as restarted after the software was changed and reloaded, the registers automatically set themselves to zero. In this case, zero was sewer penstock closed! The branch sewer penstock contently closed and the sewage in the branch sewer backed-up and eventually spilt into the waterway.

All was right with the world - it was the software engineer's fault for not resetting the registers to their appropriate value. Case closed. It was incredibly fortunate to have a contractor to blame and take the wrap!

It all sounded just a bit too convenient. After some discussion with the divisional manager we decided to have another incident debrief. The divisional manager was very keen to attend, therefore the other affected divisional managers also attended, along with all the section managers, engineers and operators – it was a packed house.

Well, it wasn't so simple after all, and a significant number of system failures occurred that contributed to the sewage spill occurrence:

- The installation procedure for the software did not include information about the "soft" registers.
- After changing the software, no-one on site – software engineers, project managers or operators, physically checked that everything was working as required. A walk around the site would have shown the penstock had closed.
- Hours before the spill, the control room operators noted in their logbook that the pumps were running slower than usual. They observed a change in operating conditions, even noted it, but no-one investigated. They had been well-informed that changes were being made on site during the day.
- The branch sewer high level alarm was on the downstream side of the penstock. This meant that it did not record the level in the branch sewer if the penstock was closed. This was a design flaw.
- The level sensor at the emergency relief structure was not monitored or alarmed to show rising levels. It was only alarmed to show when it was spilling, not give a warning that it may be about to spill.

There were a few other smaller issues, however, if any one of these circumstances had been appropriately dealt with, it was unlikely that a spill would have occurred. The results of the debrief led to major changes in the processes for how control systems were upgraded; a major review of the operations centre procedures, and a technical review of how all the monitoring was used in the system.

Most importantly, the divisional managers were able to emphasize the requirement for everyone to be alert to issues that could result in sewage spills. This one could have potentially resulted in an environmental penalty for the water authority. This would have been a very serious outcome indeed!

The first incident debrief was undertaken by the project managers who were overseeing the project. The second debrief was organised by a group of incident debrief experts outside the organisation. In my experience, the ability for groups to adequately assess their own failures is low to non-existent.

♦ ♦ ♦

Robust investigation of why things go wrong often leads to changes and awesome outcomes that reduce organisational risk. It is a good opportunity to look at situations with a wide range of people, including operators, engineers and management. It is also valuable to include some marketing and human resources people in the incident debrief as they ask questions about issues that technical staff take for granted.

It is often important to have people independent of the organisation assist in the review of the incident. They are impartial and non-judgmental in seeking to elicit information. Some organisations are emotionally insecure. This is generally observed where conflict and "scapegoating" habitually occurs between groups and within a hierarchical structure. Independent, external debriefing in these circumstances is essential to provide a "safe" environment in which the ability for individual recrimination is minimised.

Here are a few suggestions for investigating failures:

- It is always better to have someone external to the incident to manage the incident debrief. They need to be proficient at facilitation – getting participants to share information, not formulating hypotheses.
- The investigation should look at both the things that are done well and those things that could be improved.
- All people involved in the incident should be required to attend any incident debriefing. This includes external contractors and consultants.
- An action list should be developed from the investigation with nominated personnel against each action. Someone should be responsible to follow up all the actions.
- A "near misses" should be investigated as if an incident had occurred to ensure that the next time the "near miss" doesn't become a real incident.

Awesome Outcome principle:

Failure, and the lessons learned from full and frank incident investigations, can lead to more effective risk management and future awesome outcomes.

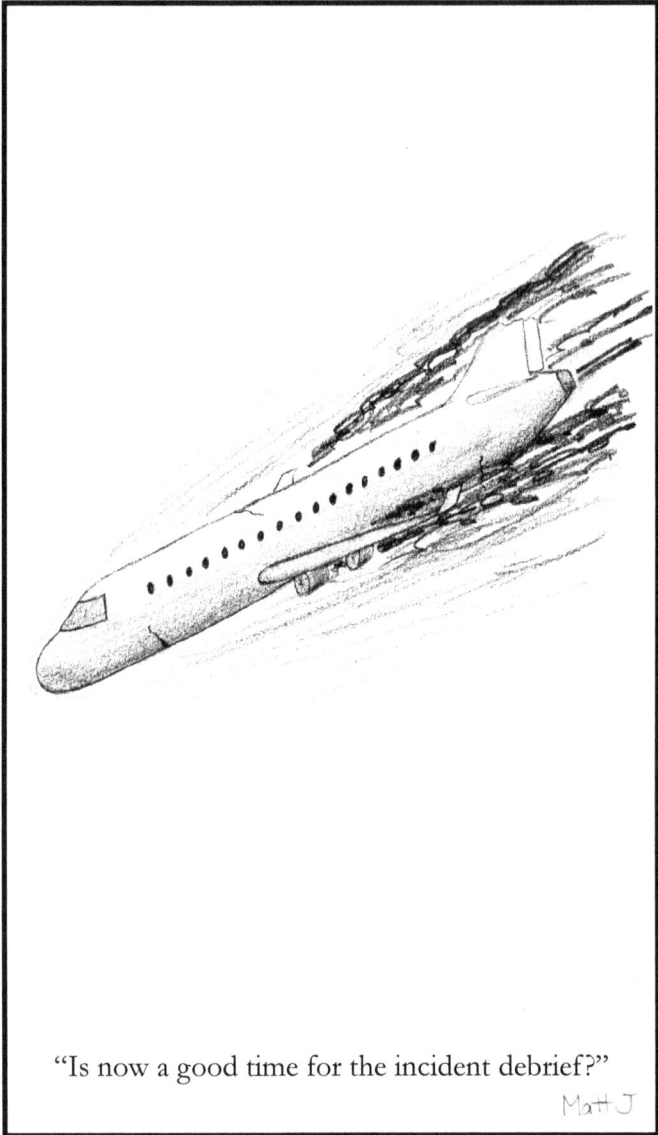

"Is now a good time for the incident debrief?"

Matt J

Post Script

As a result of this and other major incidents in the water authority, significant effort was expended on developing an incident management and debriefing system, including comprehensive implementation within the water authority. I was involved in the first training session, in which the Managing Director made sure he was a participant. This ensured that no-one had an excuse to avoid the training sessions (which ran for a few days).

The key change was to give the Incident Manager full authority to manage the incident. He or she then had "CEO" authority to procure staff, plant and equipment to fix a problem without being concerned about who had the power to request resources. If someone more senior decided they wanted to come and direct the incident management, they were offered the position of incident manager for the duration of the incident. Very few took up the kind offer!

18   Testing Assumptions

*"Your assumptions are your windows on the world.
Scrub them off every once in a while, or the light won't
come in." — Isaac Asimov*

The water authority had another large sewage treatment
plant on the other side of the city. It was the first significant sewage treatment plant for the city and its origins date
back to the nineteenth century. It was and still is a unique
plant. It has basically been a natural land and lagoon-based
treatment system with minimal energy or chemical usage.
The layout of the plant is a ride through the history of the
development of lagoon and land based treatment technology. It is also graced by a wondrous plethora of bird life and
is a major destination for migratory birds from the northern
hemisphere. It is covered by a number of international
wildlife treaties.

The plant was nearing its capacity and the water authority
was trying to determine how to upgrade the facility. The
strategy had been to build more of the same infrastructure,
which was the conservative "safe" path, but not necessarily
the most effective or efficient. This strategy had been presented to the Board for approval but was rejected as lacking
innovation.

The treatment plant manager asked if I would come and
help with the strategy. I was very busy managing the capital
works program as well as the outsourced maintenance contractor at the time. The treatment plant was more than a
two-hour drive from my home through the middle of the
city; so I was not very keen, and I declined. It was not a

decision I was very happy about – the treatment plant manager had been very good to me in my career at the water authority and I had a lot of respect for him.

Another attempt was made at the strategy, which was subsequently presented to the Board. A couple of days later, the divisional manager asked for a "chat". He explained that he had just met with the Managing Director, who had received the Board's response to the treatment strategy: a blank piece of paper, a not so subtle implication to start again from scratch. He "suggested" that I might like to help with a new strategy – an office was waiting for me at the treatment plant. A few things had happened since I had been asked previously; one of them being that I was keen to undertake some study in organisational dynamics. So I did a deal to work four days a week at the treatment plant and have a day off to undertake some study.

I had been given the impression that the strategy would only take a few weeks to develop. It didn't take long to realise that it was going to take months, especially as the silo culture was alive and well, and I would have to break it down to get a good outcome. Rather than take the office allocated to me, I sat at the vacated receptionist desk amongst the engineers and environmental scientists and made a nuisance of myself. Someone had already started work on the design of a new lagoon to match the existing ones. This had not been approved, so it was easy to bring the work to a swift end. The group eventually became a team, working towards the goal of an awesome outcome, and in the process I had repaired a relationship with one of the engineers that I thought I had permanently damaged years before.

We spent the next few months developing strategic principles for the treatment plant and investigating alternative options for its upgrade. Eventually we developed an alternative way forward; radical in its approach, but not too "out there" for a conservative government institution.

A key innovation was the review process undertaken. We set aside two days, two weeks apart, to review the strategy. We invited a vertical and horizontal cross section of the organisation to review our outcomes. Vertically, we had the divisional manager, treatment plant manager, engineers and operators from the treatment plant. Horizontally, we had my two equivalents from different parts of the organisation (water and drainage), finance, corporate strategy, research and marketing/communications representatives.

On the first day, the team presented the strategy. We limited the interaction with the reviewers to asking only clarification type questions and we asked for some general feedback at the end of the session.

Two weeks later we held the second session. We wanted the reviewers to have some time to think about the content of the strategy, even if it was only unconsciously; hence the break between the sessions was important. It is never good to presume that people read the documentation before they attend a meeting.

Here is where we broke with the traditional technical review approach. My assumption was that the people who had undertaken the technical development of the strategy were technically competent. So, in preparation, I had the team members list all the assumptions they had made in developing the strategy. There were nearly two hundred.

During the workshop we went through each assumption with the review team and quickly sorted the assumptions into those that were "given" and those that were "contestable". (As soon as someone questioned the assumption, it became contestable). The majority of the assumptions ended up being contestable. This surprised many people, as the common thought was that very few of the assumptions would be contestable.

The second step was to go through the contestable assumptions and determine which were "reasonable" and which were "debatable". To do this, the review team was broken up into small groups and fed assumptions to discuss until they were all reviewed. This took a few hours.

We ended up with about twenty assumptions that were debatable. We reconvened as a large group and went through each of the debatable assumptions and discussed whether they were critical to the outcome of the strategy and what further information was required to make them reasonable.

Over the next few weeks the strategy team did further research to consider the debatable assumptions. Once we were comfortable that none of the debatable assumptions posed a significant risk to the strategy, we developed a summary strategy which was fully accepted by the water authority. What was remarkable was that during the process, both the Managing Director and the divisional manager were replaced. However, the quality of the review process and the breadth of the review team ensured a successful result.

♦ ♦ ♦

Reflection and review are essential to development and continuous improvement. More importantly, to be able to look at things from different perspectives and to be given the opportunity to challenge assumptions and norms is the gateway to innovation and the creation of awesome outcomes.

All too often we are corralled by the herd mentality; we leave our natural curiosity and scepticism outside the front door when we come to work. This can be ingrained in organisational culture, where those who question are perceived as a destabilising influence to the organisation.

Irving L. Janis developed some important theory on "groupthink". He stated that "groupthink" is the triumph of concurrence over good sense; and authority over expertise. "Groupthink" can be found whenever organisations make difficult decisions. He considered that there were three areas that encapsulated the symptoms of "groupthink":

- Overestimation of the group. This is born out with the illusion of invulnerability, excessive optimism and extreme risk taking. There can also be an unquestioned belief in the group's inherent morality, leading to ignorance of the ethical or moral consequences of their decisions.
- Closed-mindedness. This is born out in the inability to reconsider assumptions and rationalise warnings. There can be a tendency to stereotype those who disagree as enemies or weak and stupid.
- Pressure towards uniformity. This is born out in self-censorship of deviant views and a shared illusion of unanimity. There is often direct pressure on group members to conform to consensus opinion

and self-appointed "mindguards" appear to protect the group from adverse views.

The results of "groupthink" are that few alternatives are considered, expert opinions and negative information are rejected and no contingency plans are developed.

It is the Establishment's responsibility to create safe places and processes for the review of outcomes to ensure that "groupthink" does not lead to dangerous, unpredictable results that can permanently damage or destroy an organisation.

Here are a few suggestions for testing assumptions:

- Explicitly document all the assumption made, no matter how trivial they may seem.
- Allow people time to reflect upon the implications of assumptions.
- Have as wide a group as possible to review the assumptions.
- Get people outside the technical area of competence to ask the "dumb" question. It may just be the most important one.
- Beware of "groupthink". Having territory that is forbidden to discuss can lead to a disaster. Use people outside the organisational influence to test assumptions.
- Some external agencies and consultants can be effectively embedded into the thinking of the organisation. Their independence can be compromised.

Awesome Outcome Principle:

The effective review of assumptions is critical to the acceptance of ideas and the creation of successful outcomes.

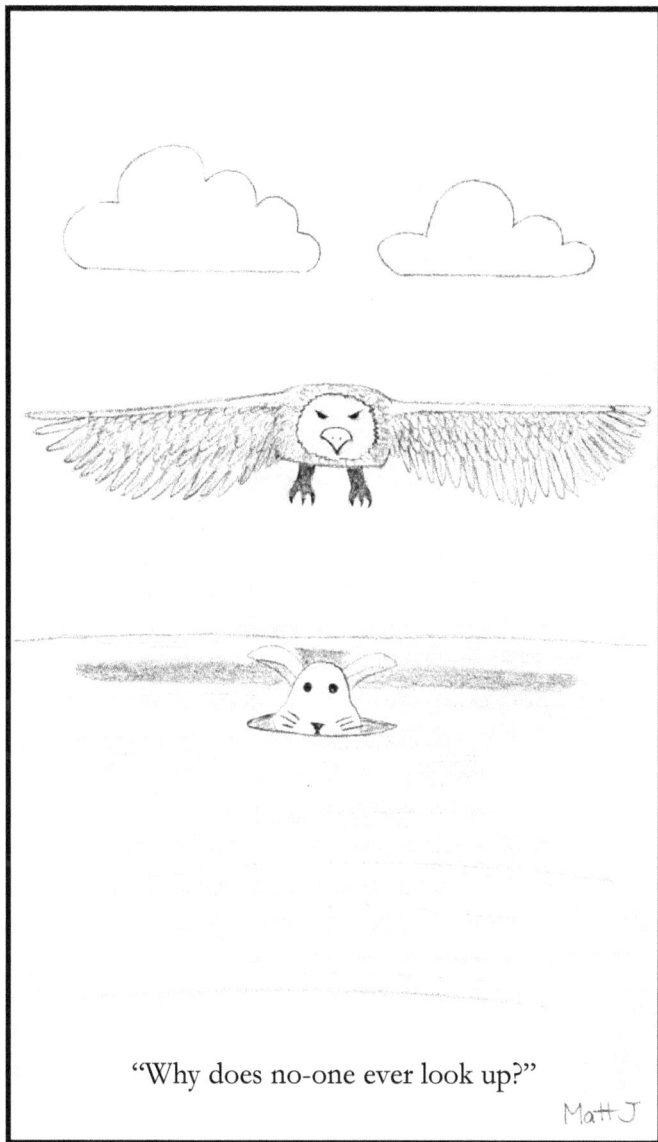

"Why does no-one ever look up?"

Post Script

While the strategy was not perfect, and I look back over some of the assumptions we made back then and cringe, the implementation provided the water authority with an efficient and effective outcome for the next fifteen years. There was so much that needed to change and we were unwilling to tackle some of the boundaries of the strategy. For example, there was a large farming business that used the property to graze cattle and sheep which was effectively excluded from the strategy review. It became difficult to undertake effective analysis as some of the strategic options altered the land usage and the viability of the farming business.

Some parts of the system also became more critical later. This did not affect the main upgrade strategy, however, not enough work was done in preparation for key issues such as water reclamation, which become a major issue as drought conditions started to affect the city.

19   Managing Risks

"I cannot imagine any condition which would cause a ship to founder. I cannot conceive of any vital disaster happening to this vessel. Modern shipbuilding has gone beyond that . . ." - Captain Edward Smith (Titanic)

I had developed a number of systems to streamline the management of the capital works program for the sewerage group, so senior management thought I wasn't busy enough. I was also requested to manage the implementation of a new maintenance services contract. The existing contract was coming to an end and a new contract needed to be developed, tendered and assessed. That was the easy part. The challenge was in managing the transition from the incumbent contractor to the new contractor without affecting the business continuity.

During the tender preparation, we visited some of the other large utilities to see how they were running their maintenance services contracts. Much of the electricity in our state is generated using brown coal excavated from large open cut mines. It is not a very environmentally sensitive way of producing electricity, but it is very cheap. The excavators are enormous and there are kilometres of conveyers to move the coal from the mine to the massive furnaces that boil water to run the electricity generators.

One of the generation companies was using a relational style of contract to manage its maintenance services. The contractor was paid for the actual cost of undertaking the maintenance services, while profit was paid in relation to the performance outcomes achieved. The client and the contractor would work together to determine the scope of work required. We spoke to the client and the contactor and they both seemed satisfied with the results they were achieving.

The water authority's contracting arrangements were very conservative. Rarely did the authority venture from fixed price contracts with conditions that were heavily biased in its own favour. I once tried to enforce some of the draconian clauses in a contract. Needless to say I only succeeded in upsetting a large number of people - project managers, the contractor and operations personnel.

The water authority had only just started outsourcing its maintenance services, and was not about to experiment on an alternative form of contracting. However, I thought the principle could be transferable to managing large capital works project – and I had just the one in mind.

The water authority was about to begin a ten year program to upgrade its largest sewage treatment plant. It was a unique plant that had been built up over the previous hundred years using mostly natural processes for the treatment of sewage. The treatment process was already unique in its configuration. The upgrade was complex and had not been attempted on this scale anywhere in the world before. It seemed a good idea to have the project managers, design engineers and constructors encouraged to work together to attempt some awesome outcomes. A relationship contracting style seemed ideal.

As can be imagined, in an organisation riddled with risk-averse engineers and accountants, the idea wasn't greeted with a great deal of enthusiasm. However, my immediate manager and the divisional manager were willing to let the idea be tested.

At this time, the water authority had an internal projects division that undertook project management services and small to medium-sized construction projects. The authority also had services contracts with some of the large consulting engineering design houses. We set up some contracts for project management and design on a relational basis. These performed well with the work being completed within the required time frame at a reasonable cost. The main advantage was that the contract payment terms encouraged the water authority personnel and the engineering consultant personnel to collaborate more effectively. (I also had the authority personnel performance bonuses linked to the same performance outcomes as the consultants!) These were relatively inexpensive non-critical works, so the risk to the water authority was minimal.

We also needed to test the construction phase, which was ten times the cost of design, with greater opportunity for things to go wrong. We decided to set up two contracts with the internal construction group to test the contracting idea. The first contract was a complex relining of a large ovoid (egg shaped) sewer where every section of the lining was different. The sewer followed a major road through a significant shopping precinct, requiring major public communication and consultation. The second contract was a large recycled water pipeline through open fields. Both the sewer and the pipeline were large enough for people to walk (crawl maybe) through, so they were sizeable construction contracts.

I will never cease to be amazed at how hard people work on complex jobs and end up with awesome outcomes. The contract team undertaking the sewer lining were continually coming up with new ways to place the lining pieces. The job was completed months earlier than expected, significantly under budget and with very few community complaints. The project team tracked the number of sections laid every day and there was a steady increase over the length of the project. They set themselves some outlandish targets, which I don't think they met, but they came very close. There is a concept called exponential learning that applies to these types of projects. If you allow the team to be creative in the way it undertakes its work, it will take half the time to do the first quarter of the work, but the last quarter will be done in one tenth of the time!

It also never ceases to amaze me at how relatively simple jobs can go awfully wrong. The recycled water pipeline was laid in record time – with only one problem. When the pipe was pressure tested, it leaked at every joint. The sealing rubber rings between the pipe sections had been incorrectly installed (bit like the space shuttle Challenger without the devastating consequences). Every joint needed to be resealed – making the project late and over budget.

Although the contract was poorly executed, the fundamentals of the contract were solid enough not to expose the water authority to serious risk. We made a slight change to the contract requiring that major rework be undertaken at the cost of the contractor. The contractor had already lost most of the performance payment due to lateness and cost overruns.

Having a poor performing contract that did not expose the water authority to increased risk was a blessing in disguise. There was sufficient evidence to show that the contracting methodology was robust enough for implementation. It took over two years to convince the water authority to undertake the work using a relational style contract. A large proportion of the water authority's contract work is now undertaken in a relational form.

♦ ♦ ♦

It takes faith to undertake innovation and challenge the status quo, but blind faith is a recipe for disaster. It should not be innovation at all costs, but carefully structured changes where the risks and consequences of failure are clearly managed.

The investigation of the space shuttle Challenger explosion indicated that the main cause of the accident was the ignorance of technical issues by senior management whose primary concern was to launch the spacecraft instead of investigating the reasons why it should not be launched.

Apparently, the ancient Romans had a novel method for managing the risks associated with the construction of their bridges. Once the bridges were built, they would get the design engineer and the builder to stand underneath the bridge. Then the army commanders would command the army to march across the bridge. Nothing like an incentive to get a job done well!

Here are a few suggestions for managing risks:

- Understand the risks involved in a project.
- Own the risks – don't try and push them onto others.
- Minimise the consequences of failure – trying to remove risks will inevitably lead to maintaining the status quo, which is a risky strategy in itself.
- Get independent, credible experts to review the project. Make sure there are minimal "noddies" in the review team and encourage robust discussion.
- Discuss the project with those who will end up operating and managing the outcome – often they will see things the "experts" miss.
- Create a culture of rewarding effort, not penalising failure.
- Test concepts and ideas before full scale implementation.
- Have a back-up plan.

Awesome Outcome Principle:

The risks associated with innovation require testing to ensure that awesome outcomes are achieved.

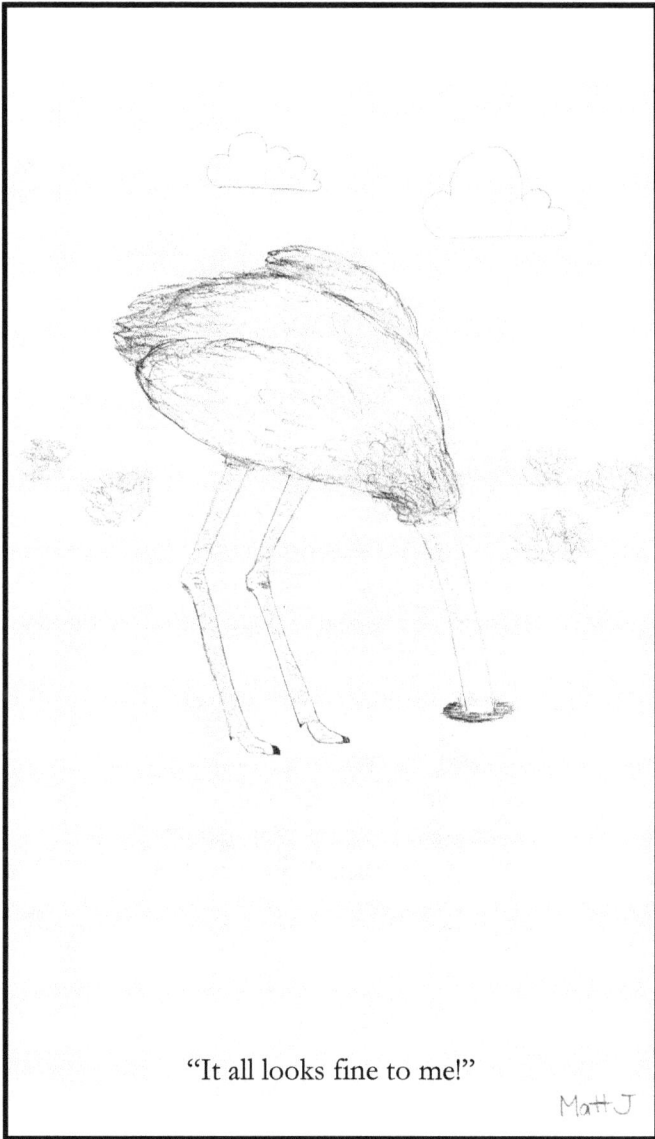

"It all looks fine to me!"

Matt J

Post Script

The major works at the treatment plant were undertaken using a relational contract that had three performance measures – time, cost and outcome, which in this case was the amount of nitrogen that was removed from the treated sewage. The weighting of each performance component was apportioned in relation to the ability of the team member to influence the outcome. The process designer was heavily weighted on treatment outcome, while the constructer was heavily weighted on time and cost.

Quality, which is often subjective and difficult to quantify, was managed differently. The project consisted of multiple process units to be constructed over a period of five years. The performance contracts were non-exclusive. That is, no party was guaranteed to get the next portion of work in the construction sequence. It was at the absolute discretion of the water authority. If any member of the team was not performing, the water authority could replace them for the next piece of work.

These types of contracts take a great deal of emotional energy. They require significant communication, good-will and patience. The project managers struggled with this, and every now and then they would suggest that the next stage of the project should be undertaken using "traditional" fixed price contracts.

20 Mavericks on the Dark Side

"What a group as a whole deem to be true and just, becomes true and just. Anyone who does not think like the group is excluded, driven off, killed or declared mad." – Janine Chasseguer-Smirgel

I had decided to test and develop my management skills by moving out of the water industry and successfully procured a management position within the telecommunications industry. My role was to manage the physical telecommunications infrastructure network for a large metropolitan city. The organisation was looking for ways to more effectively and efficiently undertake their work, so part of my role was to identify and implement changes to create a more productive workplace.

They were having significant problems with installing enough infrastructure (copper wires) to connect customers in a timely manner. A number of "innovative" interventions had been undertaken by senior management to address the rising number of unconnected customers. It was becoming clear that while the number of unconnected customers had decreased during the "interventions", it quickly "recovered" to its increasing rate of disconnectedness. Clearly the strategies were not working, but no-one was willing to undertake the forensic work to determine the effectiveness of the interventions.

I met with a number of the other team leaders to discuss the issues. These meetings were intense, and it was often difficult to get agreement on who was accountable for what tasks. We undertook workshops with our staff and discussed the resulting issues with the section manager in the monthly team leaders meeting. We decided that one of the key problems was the workplace structure and accountabilities. We suggested that a discussion needed to be held with the divisional manager at our next managers' meeting.

The following team leader's meeting with the divisional manager was a disaster. The divisional manager started drawing circles on a white board and espousing his management theory. "The white space between the circles is unclear accountabilities – it's your job (team leaders) to manage this". Then the "blame game" started – with most of the blame being attributed to the lack of will of the general staff to work more efficiently. I had always been taught that clear accountabilities were the essence of good management, which was at odds with the divisional manager's view of management. I naively told him so, which was definitely a career limiting move.

◆ ◆ ◆

One difficulty that the Establishment has with Mavericks is how to manage a Maverick's often highly sensitive moral compass. This can often be seen with those who have instigated great social change.-William Wilberforce and the abolition of slavery in England; Ghandi and the liberation of India from the British; Martin Luther King and the civil rights movement in the United States and Nelson Mandela and the dismantling of Apartheid in South Africa. Each one saw their nation as more than the culmination of the existing government policy. They understood that the ideals of a nation should be accessible to all the peoples within the nation. Mavericks are those that often see their organisation as more than an accumulation of corporate policies.

They see the organisation as a place for meaningful work and efficient and effective outcomes.

Good Mavericks are a rare breed. They are often extremely difficult to manage, intense and have good analytical skills. They can envision the ultimate outcome required, and a practical path for it to be achieved. I heard a Maverick described once as someone who had their head in the clouds with both feet planted firmly on the ground. Most importantly, they have a knack for transposing ideas from one context to another to create awesome outcomes.

Mavericks often think outside the management stream and generally look at what they think is best to improve the organisational outcomes. Sometimes the Establishment is more concerned with managing anxiety or the enhancement of individual egos, rather than achieving awesome outcomes. In these cases there is often conflict between the Establishment and the Mavericks and outcomes are nearly always compromised. The Maverick does not often does survive the process. Only rarely do they become the Managing Director.

As an example of Establishment interference, I once employed an extremely capable engineer who would fit the Maverick characterisation well. We had worked together in a previous incarnation of the water authority and I still have a high regard for him. However, just before we were about to engage him, I had a phone call from my divisional manager. One of his colleagues had suggested that this engineer was a bit of a "troublemaker". I assured the divisional manager that while the engineer was sometimes difficult to manage, I had always known him to seek to do what he thought was best for the water authority. He trusted my judgement and we employed him. The engineer was sometimes difficult to manage, and many intense discussions were undertaken, but the difference he made to the team's ability to be creative and develop awesome outcomes cannot be overstated.

Exceptional Mavericks have the ability to bring out and encourage the maverick skills within the Workers. Supreme Mavericks can do it without incurring the wrath of the Establishment!

Here are a few suggestions for managing Mavericks:

- If no-one is challenging the status quo, there are no effective Mavericks. They will exist in the organisation; they are just keeping their heads low to avoid decapitation.
- Too many Mavericks spoil the organisation. People can only cope with a finite amount of challenges to the status quo.
- There is a time for challenge and a time for moving on. Mavericks need to learn that once the status quo has been questioned and the Establishment makes a decision, it's time to move on.
- If a senior manager often uses the term "trouble-maker", it is probably time to replace the senior manager.
- Importing Mavericks on short term contracts or as consultants can be very effective.

Awesome Outcome Principle:

To create a stable, outcome focused organisation the Establishment must encourage Mavericks, while protecting the Workers from overzealousness and ineptitude.

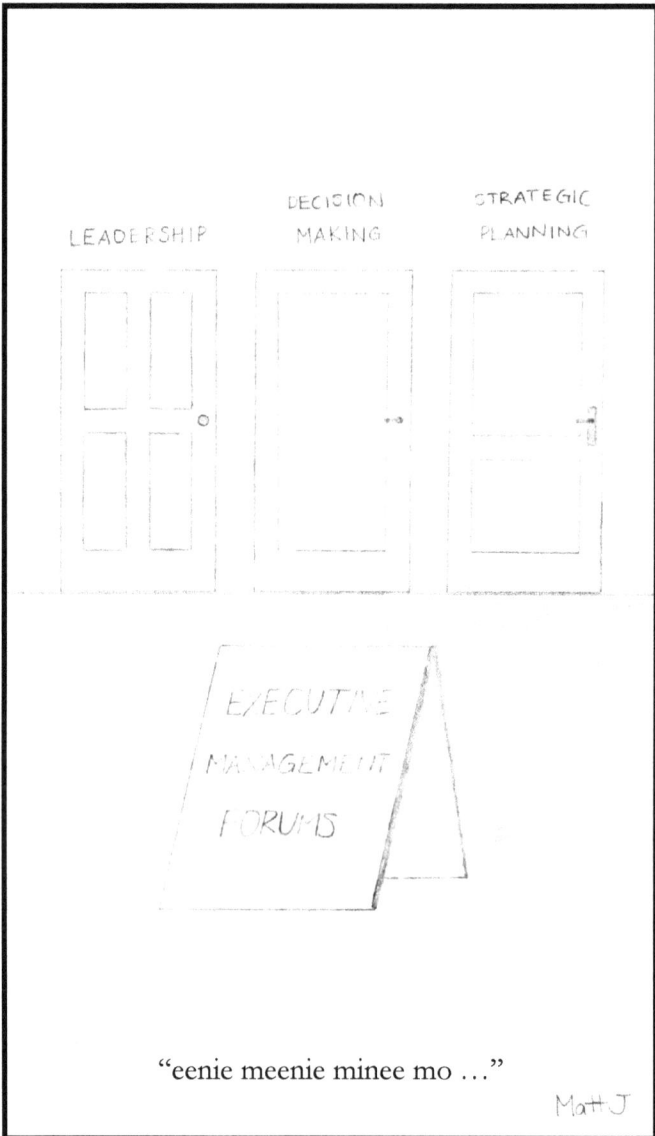

"eenie meenie minee mo …"

Post Script

At the telecommunications organisation I clearly took on the role of the Maverick. I was not only an outsider to the organisation, but also to the industry. I had come from a water industry that had undergone significant change and I was young and overly enthusiastic. I was also under the impression that I had a mandate to instigate change.

The problem was the Establishment considered that change only needed to occur at the Worker level, and having some "outsider" question the way the organisation was run was unacceptable. It may not be surprising to hear that the share price of the company dropped significantly over the following years. It is also not surprising that I was killed off quickly!

21 Enabling Others

> *"But of a good leader, who talks little, when the job is done, they all say 'we did it ourselves'."- Lao Tzu*

Organisations often espouse the objective of enabling others to develop more efficient ways of working. In reality this is very difficult to achieve. The need for managers to be seen to be in control often overrides the desire to create an open working environment. It is also difficult to maintain within an underbounded environment without correcting the imbedded governance issues.

The water authority decided to implement a cultural change program based on the "self-managed teams" approach. The aim was to allow staff to manage how their tasks were undertaken to achieve the outcomes within the boundaries set by the management. I was managing the planning group at one of the major sewage treatment plant at the time. We were a long way, both physically and culturally, from the head office and the divisional offices. We had the opportunity to try out new ways of working without too much scrutiny. (The divisional manager once lamented that he considered our group to be feral – but could do little about it as we were achieving the business requirements).

We needed to recruit more engineers into the group, so in line with the "self-managed team" approach, the recruitment process was altered to include a team interview of any potential new staff. The team was given veto power if they thought the person did not fit the team – or where there were multiple acceptable candidates, to choose the preferred candidate. My view of self-management was, and still is, not anarchy, but delegating decisions in a controlled environment.

The interview process decided by the team was quite novel and I was also invited to attend the interview with the team. Someone baked a cake to share at the interview. Each team member introduced themselves and explained their role in the team. The initial questions were those common sense riddles (if an electric train travelling north is buffeted by an easterly wind, which way does the smoke blow!?). This was followed by some general chit-chat and some discussion of the person's experience and capabilities. When the interview was finished, I took the interviewee out of the room. The team members then had a discussion about whether or not the candidate was suitable for the team. The whole process took about an hour.

This was one of those innovations that ended up with some awesome outcomes. Once the team had decided that the potential member was a good fit, they eagerly took responsibility for the new team member's arrival. Desks were rearranged. Security gate passes and computers were sorted out. The new employees felt like they were part of the team before they arrived and were eager to get down to some work.

What became clear was that the team were mostly concerned about how the new member would fit into the group and what complimentary skills they had to offer. They tended to trust the process undertaken to get the person to be a preferred candidate, so they focused on the interaction skills of the candidate.

◆ ◆ ◆

There is a notion regarding team building that the term "empowering" is a misnomer. What organisations really do is disempower their staff for the sake of efficiency, order and control – and in pathological organisations, pander to the Establishment's low self-esteem. To make matters worse, employees allow themselves to be disempowered. Often people, who in everyday life are creative and make sensible and rational decisions, regress in their workplaces to sheep and sometimes lemmings, eager to follow each other off some organisational cliff.

It takes courage for the Establishment to delegate responsibility and believe that people will take on the responsibility with the same determination. However, taking on responsibility and achieving awesome outcomes can be very infectious. Work places can start implementing rapid change through innovative ideas that come from the ground up, especially if they are practical and make sense.

There is a saying used in development circles that goes something like this. "Give a person a fish, feed them for a day, teach a person to fish, feed them for life." I think the analogy can be extended further. "Give a person the skills and opportunity to develop new ways to fish and they can feed the whole village".

I was told a story some years ago that illustrates this. An aid organisation had some money they wanted to invest into a remote village in South America. They wanted to use the empowerment principle to let the people in the village decide how the money should be spent. The development workers sat down with the villagers and asked them what they wanted. The villagers were keen to have a new road built. The development workers thought this was a bad idea. They were afraid that a road would erode the peaceful village culture by allowing undesirables to come in. So they suggested new water systems, toilets, improved agricultural techniques – but the people were adamant they wanted a road.

The development workers stuck with their empowerment principle and arranged for a road to be built. There was a lot of opposition from surrounding villages, but the people pressed on with the road, even after some of their workers had been killed by bandits.

The problem for the villagers was getting their produce to markets. The narrow passes in the mountains made it difficult to transport goods. Many of the passes had bandits and landowners who required "tolls" to be paid to pass through (hence the resistance to the construction of road). The villages had already figured out that if they could sell their goods in the nearby city, they could buy all the other things the development workers were offering.

Here are a few suggestions for empowerment:
- Set clear boundaries for allowing others to make decisions.
- Provide access to appropriate resources to enable good decisions to be made.
- Introduce team members to other parts of the organisation and to senior management. Allow team members to test their ideas with these people.
- Allow decisions to be followed through, even if the managers are not convinced they will work. Managers are not all-knowing, and can sometimes be pleasantly surprised. Make sure the team has a back-up plan if the idea doesn't work out.
- Where team decisions have to be overruled, make sure the reasons are clearly articulated.

Awesome Outcome Principle:

Enabling others to use their creativity and empowering them to implement their ideas can create awesome outcomes.

"Not sure he will catch much there!"

Matt J

Post Script

I have had a few discussions with those new employees in later years. They described how confronted they felt when they entered the room to be interviewed by such a large group, but when they left they very much wanted to be a part of the team. One of them still works with me now.

It is important to say a few words regarding the nexus between the underbounded nature in the organisation and the use of "self-managed teams". It basically failed, and the lesson is found in the exception. When I started with this group, there were so many problems that I took away nearly all opportunities for the staff to make decisions. I knew nothing about the over/underbounded concept. I just knew things were very wrong. Not a single piece of correspondence left the group without my approval.

As we set up appropriate governance processes, the tight management was relaxed, and I was no longer working such long days. When the "self-managed teams" approach came, the team was able to embrace the concept knowing full well what the expectations and boundaries were. Most other groups did not go through this process. Some did not see the value in it. They were already doing what they wanted to do, and struggled with the concept of setting boundaries. Some groups were stuck in the process of moving from being underbounded to overbounded.

22 Developing Mentors

"Tell me and I forget, teach me and I may remember, involve me and I learn" – Benjamin Franklin

Over the years I have been blessed with wonderful mentors in both my personal and professional life. As a graduate engineer I joined a large multidisciplinary engineering consultancy. It was a private company, with share ownership by Principals and Associates who were practising engineers. It had a very flat management structure in which all employees were generally responsible to one of the Principals.

Access to people was determined by need and expertise. A new graduate was expected to approach the best expert in the company to gain advice on an issue, even if that person was the Managing Director. The internal culture was such that approaches by junior staff to senior staff were generally welcomed. Within this context, I had access to some very experienced professionals. I was also in the unique position to know what a personal computer was, and how to competently program. It is hard to comprehend these days; but the office only had one large mainframe computer with three terminals that were mostly used by the hydrological section. There was a typing pool that typed up all our correspondence and reports. They had just acquired an IBM XT personal commuter with an Excel spreadsheet. On my first day I was told to stay away from it in case I broke it.

As the senior engineers realised that I could do sophisticated hydraulic modelling on the computer, I was asked to be involved in larger and more complex projects. I had to buy my own personal computer for my desk and paid it off by writing hydraulic software for the company in my spare time. This may sound strange, but I was a civil engineer and, even though I had an aptitude for using computers, I wanted to be more involved in practical work – making a difference to the community I live in. I made a point of not writing software during working hours, so I would be involved in engineering. Not the most profitable of choices, but satisfying, and one I have never regretted.

I was able to work with some great people and will break with my general writing style and mention three by name – Colin Mews, Lindsay Mott and Nick Apostolidis. Each had a significant influence on my professional development.

Colin "the Captain" Mews is a passionate sailor and an extraordinary engineer. He is one of those people who doesn't suffer fools, but is very approachable and I greatly enjoyed working with him. He has hundreds of stories. He is also an expert in contract formation and the management of contracts. I worked with him to help rewrite the engineering specifications sections for all of the company contract documentation.

Lindsay "the Professor" Mott is a passionate engineer, who is one of those "outside of the square" ideas people. Whatever project he worked on, he tried new ideas to make it either work better or be more economical. He was always seeking the help of others to not only verify that his ideas would work, but to improve and optimise the performance. He often became so engrossed in solving problems at work that he sometimes forgot to go home. He would be designing pumping stations in all kinds of unusual places and unusual configurations, and I sometimes developed a model to show that it could work. Most of these models were computer based, but on one occasion we built a one tenth scale working model in a laboratory at the neighbouring university.

Nick "the Greek" Apostolidis is passionate about his heritage and his engineering. I remember when he became a Principal; he walked around the office proudly stating that he was the first Greek Principal of the company. He was an expert at convincing clients to implement innovative solutions. He was often the one that "sold" Lindsay's ideas. He was one of the few senior engineers that had a good grasp of computer modelling, and we worked together on some sophisticated models for water, drainage and sewage networks. He also developed a significant part of the business relating to infiltration into sewage networks.

All three were, in their own ways, Mavericks. They were not very good at compromise; they wanted excellence in everything they were involved in. They were all passionate – although Colin would never admit that he was passionate about anything else but sailing. I regard each of them as great early mentors who made significant time for my innumerable questions. There were many others, the company had many brilliant engineers, but these three stand out, mostly because they were willing to work with my eccentric and intense manner. They were also great story tellers.

◆ ◆ ◆

Creating awesome outcomes is about moulding ideas to meet the current situation. Having mentors allows ideas to be tested by people who have the wisdom of age and experience. This is the quality of sagacity – one that is often lost in the western world's preoccupation with youth and formal education. You can teach someone how to design a bridge, but it takes experience, and sometimes failure, to create new ways of working and solving some of the unique situations that are encountered.

Learning from failure and changing the way we work so it doesn't happen again is an extraordinary experience. As Albert Einstein quaintly observed: "the definition of insanity is doing the same thing over and over again and expecting different results"

Often we look to the high flyers, like Richard Branson and Steve Jobs, for inspiration and see them as mentors. They are inspirational, but our best mentors are going to be people in our own organisations, mainly because they are accessible. They have a wealth of experience and stories to tell, if we are willing to listen.

Here are a few suggestions for developing good mentors:

- Find people who are respected for what they achieve, not how they look or speak. "Charismatic" mentors might feel good to be around, but may not give the best practical advice.
- Mentors who are passionate about what they do are worth more than gold.
- Good mentors will give you critical feedback that may not be comfortable, but in the long run will be very helpful.
- The most unlikely people can make excellent mentors. I once worked for a manager whose people skills were not the best, but he was an excellent administrator. I still use much of what I learned from him to run my own business today.
- Have a diverse group of mentors. As I was growing up, three of my mentors came from very different backgrounds, but I respected each of them very much. One was a PhD engineering student, one was a fitter and turner and one was a chef. They came from very different walks of life, and had quite different world views, but I enjoyed my time with each of them immensely.

Awesome Outcome Principle:

Finding passionate mentors is a key to developing awesome outcomes.

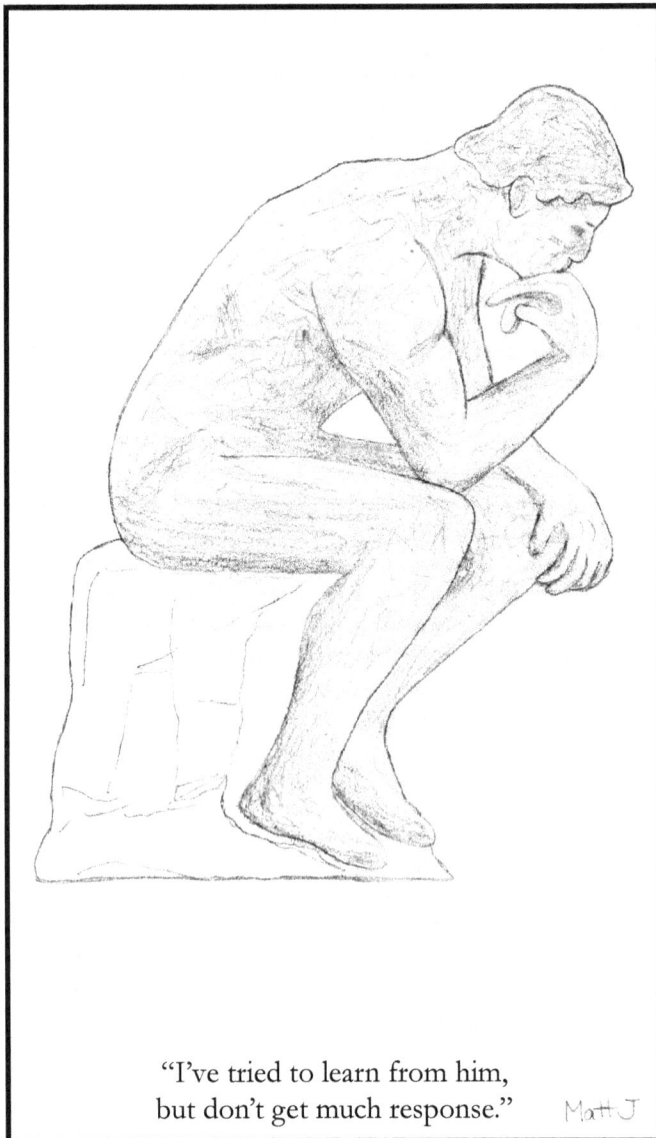

"I've tried to learn from him,
but don't get much response."

Matt J

Post Script

I have a role in an organisation as the "wandering mentor". I spend a day a month walking around the office, talking to staff, telling stories and giving some general advice on the problems they are encountering. Some of the staff perceive me as a nuisance, some as a sounding board for ideas, and some see me as a breath of fresh air. I encourage individuals to take some of their issues up with senior management, and other issues they will just have to grin and bear.

I am very careful not to act as a mediator between the Establishment and the Workers. However, sometimes I see systemic issues in the workplace and take these up with the management directly. The Middle Managers are the ones that have the most difficulty with my role, mostly because their ability to control what I say or do is minimal.

23 Reflection

Throughout this narrative, I have touched on my experience and understanding of how people within organisations can create awesome outcomes and not get bound by the status quo. Challenging the status quo in itself is not the means by which we create effective change. The Maverick is neither a good or bad agent for change. Change for the sake of doing things differently does not necessarily lead to awesome outcomes.

It is important to try and discern the real reasons for wanting change, both conscious and unconscious, and have a clear understanding of the outcomes desired. There is no easy way to do this, and dealing with the darker sides of our organisations and ourselves can be extremely challenging.

I have found the concept of the Johari window to be very helpful in understanding what we know of ourselves and the world around us and how others perceive us.

Consider a house with four rooms as a two-by-two matrix.

Along the horizontal axis we have self-knowledge – what we know about ourselves and what we do not know.

On the vertical axis we have others knowledge - what they know about us and what they do not know.

Self-knowledge

	Known	Unknown
Known	Open	Blind Spot
Unknown	Hidden	Unconscious

Others Knowledge

Johari Window

The **Open room** is what we know about ourselves and others know as well – it is our public space. It includes physical things, such as eye colour and public preferences, like our favourite food. From an organisational perspective it includes things such as the corporate image, logos and so on.

The **Hidden room** is what we know about ourselves that is not known by others – it is our private space. It often includes thing like our fears and secret desires. From an organisational perspective it includes things such as trade secrets.

The **Blind Spot room** is what others know about us that we don't know – it is our unaware space. It often includes our habits and behavioural perceptions. It can also include strengths and weaknesses that we are unaware of, and often our prejudices. From an organisational perspective it includes unknown customer preferences and issues.

The **Unconscious room** is what neither we nor others know about us – it is our unconscious space. It often includes the rationale for why we behave in ways that seem irrational. It may be physiological – such as a blood clot that is causing memory loss, or psychological, such as a childhood trauma that creates anxiety when similar circumstances are encountered. From an organisational perspective, it includes social defence systems, where unconscious behaviour affects the way in which people in the organisation relate.

All four rooms make up the house and affect the emotional balance of how the house operates. The more we operate in the open room, the more effective we can be at improving the way we work. This applies to the individual, the group and the organisation as a whole.

To move from the Hidden to the Open, we need to develop credibility and a belief in ourselves that can be greatly enhanced through creating an enabling culture within an organisation.

To move from the Blind Spot to the Open, we need to intrinsically value ourselves and allow for the critical review of what we do through robust discussions and the creation of quality mentors.

Organisations can be schizophrenic when dealing with these two rooms. The objective is to find a good balance between positive reinforcement and critical review. When organisations focus on the hidden, it is nearly impossible for people to discover their blind spots. This can be detrimental to relationships within the organisation as people become oblivious to their impact on others. It can also lead to an unhealthy dependency on positive reinforcement for personal value.

Conversely, when the focus is on the blind spots, people find it difficult to reveal information about themselves, in particular the evaluation of strengths and weaknesses. This can be detrimental to an individual's feeling of self-worth and can lead to withdrawal and introspection (flight) or open aggression (fight).

Reflecting on the unconscious

The unconscious is possibly the most difficult and potentially dangerous room in the house. It will affect the way we behave and undertake our activities, but we will not be able to understand the rationale surrounding the behaviour. This is where the shadows stir, and the potential for self-destructive and pathological behaviour reside.

Mostly, we can only guess at the things that reside within this room, however, a way to improve our understanding of our behaviour is through reflection. One of my poor social habits is interrupting people when they are talking to me. While I can speculate that one of the reasons for this is my upbringing (growing up in a household with three females that never stopped talking), there are probably some deep-seated anxieties that sit within my unconscious so that no-one really understands why I do it. No matter how hard I try not to do it, there are occasions when I will interrupt what others are saying.

One of the methods that I have used to help me with this is reflection. More importantly, it is to reflect on how I feel when I interrupt other people. The aim is to recognise the feeling of anxiety before I interrupt others and try not to interrupt what they are saying. Over the years I have become better at recognising when I get to this position – at least I recognise when I have done it and can make amends for the rudeness.

There is often a great fear in organisations to reflect on the way it undertakes tasks, and how the process may affect the behaviour of those who undertake the tasks. All too often the focus is on the behaviour rather than the anxiety caused by the task.

Double Loop Learning

Chris Argris and Donald Schon have developed the concept of double loop learning, which has become the basis of reflective practice. Single loop learning is the standard Plan-Do-Review model. We set goals or objectives, sometimes unconsciously, and then plan what tasks are required to meet them. We do the tasks and review the outcomes against the desired goal. If we are diligent, we alter how we undertake the tasks to be more effective and efficient in meeting the goals. This is a continuous process for continuous improvement.

Double Loop Learning adds a second loop of reflection around setting the goals and objectives. This requires critical reflection of the underlying assumptions in determining and resetting the goals. To be effective we also need to realise that the underlying assumptions come from all four rooms of the house. External assistance is often required to understand the assumptions that spring from the blind spot and unconscious. This process takes significant emotional energy and can only be effectively applied at discrete intervals. Undertaken too often, it can cause organisational change fatigue, while if spread too far apart can heighten the risk of organisational failure.

Security and Significance

Finally, I believe that we all need to understand what gives us significance and what gives us security. The degree of significance and security that we require will depend on many factors – race, gender, social culture and so on. I do not believe that these can be given, but ultimately have to found, which is where the positive reinforcement school of thinking comes undone. If individuals or organisations are unwilling or unable to seek and accept critical evaluation of their strengths and weaknesses, the ability to utilise or strengthen these areas is diminished. Through reflection we come to realisation, and a sober understanding of our value to those around us. This is linked to the psychological concept of self-efficacy.

It is not the organisation's responsibility to provide security and significance for people, but it is important to provide an environment that enables individuals to feel safe, both physically and emotionally, and develop meaningful and useful work. I firmly believe that any organisation that works hard to create a safe environment for the Maverick in all of us to prosper will create a platform for innovation and the potential for awesome outcomes.

"Too much creativity, not enough reflection."

Matt J

24 Epilogue

My father was never one to accept the status quo. He was trained as a primary school teacher and started teaching in remote rural schools where the total number of students rarely exceeded thirty. The ability to improvise and innovate was essential as these schools were generally poorly resourced and there were no support staff to help with the administration.

He was taught early how to bend the rules. A family day was held at one of these schools and someone provided a keg of beer. The Education Department rulebook did not allow alcohol on school premises, and, wanting to do the right thing, he went to explain the difficulty to the keg provider. The "no worries" response was to place the keg over the fence on the footpath outside the school property. Problem solved!

After starting a family he returned to the city and made his way through the teaching ranks, gaining credibility in his chosen profession. He worked hard to create a sense of community amongst his colleagues. I remember BBQs and film nights with his fellow teachers in our backyard at home when we were growing up. He eventually made his way to School Principal, a role that was mostly administrative but he always tried to take time out to teach a few classes a week to maintain his expertise and relevance.

He was extremely proficient at bending the rules to achieve awesome outcomes. I remember him sharing the story of how his school was one of the first to have computers for students. The Education Department had allocated money to resurface the outside basketball court at the school. The local council just happened to be re-sealing the roads around the school. Having the presence of mind and an excellent understanding of the currency commonly found in the local economy ("slabs" of beer), he convinced the construction workers to make a detour and resurface the basketball court. Thus the money for the basketball court went to purchase computers.

His first role as a Principal was at a new school that was using an experimental method of teaching. Not only did he have to encourage the staff in the new way of teaching, he also had to learn how to manage a school. These were a difficult few years, and being someone who does not suffer fools gladly, he had to manage the inevitable conflicts that come with innovation and change. Following a restructuring of the Education Department, he decided to go back to classroom teaching at a larger school.

It did not take long for him obtain another position as Principal. For over ten years he was dedicated to improving a school in a not-so-well-off outer suburban area. The school was difficult to manage, with numerous problems related to the lower socio-economics of the community. Despite this, the teachers developed strong accountable relationships, and he often reminisced over some of the awesome outcomes they achieved.

The Education Department was a bureaucratic monolith full of shadows and silos and he avoided dealing with it as much as practically possible. It finally became too much to tolerate, and when the Department went on an "economy" drive, my father took an early retirement package. It always seemed a bit sad to me that the Education Department was not able to use his experience to improve education. I think my father had challenged the status quo so much over the years that they were both glad to see the back of each other.

He was able to use his administrative and logistic skills to be gainfully employed helping his mates move factories, clerking for a lawyer, running a small business, assisting with managing state and federal elections and finally helping me set up the administration for my consulting business. Sadly, he had nothing more to do with educating young people (except for maybe his grandchildren).

◆ ◆ ◆

The ability of organisations to successfully use Mavericks is a key to the development and implementation of innovative ideas and the creation of awesome outcomes. The ability of Mavericks to develop appropriate expertise, work together with Middle Managers, gain credibility with the Establishment and convince organisations to undertake change is a measure of their skill and perseverance. This requires organisations to encourage robust discussions and develop accountable relationships amongst individuals and work groups.

Organisations must be willing to be challenge the status quo if they want to achieve awesome outcomes. They need to be willing to delve into their shadows, break down the silos and fix the structures that inhibit change. They need to develop an effective management hierarchy, within a well-bounded culture that sets direction, but does not constrain creativity. Above all, avoidance of mediocrity and the development of a collaborative culture that works for the good of the organisation will produce awesome outcomes.

They also need to create the transitional space to allow people within the organisations to farewell the old ways of doing things and eagerly take up the new. This also includes some time in the confusion room, where some of the shadows can be worked through, even though the outcome may not be perfectly clear.

All innovation and change involves taking risks and these risks need to be acknowledged, owned and managed by the Establishment. Allowing Mavericks to implement innovation without assessing the risks and having back-up plans is a recipe for disaster. However, when things go wrong, a well-structured, independent incident debrief can lead to significant organisational improvement.

Finally, the importance of sharing stories, the development of good mentors and the ability to reflect and allow others to critique the way we work together will allow individuals to grow and mature and make a difference to the way organisations achieve their goals.

Further Reading

Alderfer, C P and Cooper, C L (1980), *Advances in Experiential Social Processes, Volume 2.* John Wiley & Sons

Allport, G (1954) *The Nature of Prejudice.* Doubleday, New York

Ambrose, A (1989) *Key concepts of the transitional approach to managing change.* In Klein, L (ed.) *Working with organisations.* Published privately

Argris, C and Schon, D (1978) *Organisational Learning: A Theory of Action Perspective.* Reading, MA Addison-Wesley

Ashby, W R (1960) *An introduction to Cybernetics.* Chapman & Hall, London

Bain, A (1998) *Social defences against organisational learning.* Human Relations, Vol. 51, No. 3

Bakan, J (2004) *The pathological pursuit of profit and power.* Free Press, New York

Bandura, A (1977) *Social Learning Theory.* Englewood Cliffs, NJ: Prentice Hall

Banuazizi, A & Movahedi, S (1975) *Interpersonal dynamics in a simulated prison: A methodological analysis. American Psychologist, 30,* 152-160

Bion, W R (1961) *Experience in Group.* Tavistock Publications , London

Bridges, W (1991) *Managing transition.* Massachusetts, Addison-Wesley Publishing Company

Chamorro-Premuzic, T (2013) *Does Money Really Affect Motivation? A Review of the Research.* Harvard Business Review April 2013

de Board, R (1978) *The Psychoanalysis of Organisations.* Routledge, London

de Bono, E (1985) *Six Thinking Hats: An Essential Approach to Business Management.* Little, Brown, & Company

Dingle, T and Rasmussen, C (1991) *Vital Connections: Melbourne and its Board of Works 1891-1981.* Penguin Books, Australia

Drucker, P (1954) *The Practice of management.* Perennial Library, New York

Fettweis, C J (2013) *The pathologies of power.* Cambridge University Press

Ferraris, C and Carveth, R (2003), *NASA and the Columbia Disaster: Decision-making by Groupthink.* Proceedings of the 2003 Association for Business Communication Annual Convention. Association for Business Communication

Goldsworthy, A (2003) *The complete Roman army.* Thames & Hudson

Gray, P (2011) *Psychology.* Worth Publishers

Haney, C, Banks, C, & Zimbardo, P (1973) *Interpersonal dynamics in a simulated prison. International Journal of Criminology & Penology, 1*(1), 69-97

Hirschhorn, L (1988) *The workplace within.* MIT Press, Cambridge

Hitchings, B (1979) *West Gate.* Outback Press

Hockley, R (1996) *In the wake of change - A demonstration workshop and process guidelines for senior managers and experienced change practitioners.* Unpublished

Huff, J L (2001) *Parental attachment, reverse culture shock, perceived social support, and college adjustment of missionary children.* - Journal of Psychology & Theology 29.3 (2001): 246-264.29 Sept 2009.Web

Janis, I (1982) *Victims of Groupthink.* Boston: Houghton Mifflin

Jung, C G (1968) *The archetypes and the collective unconscious.* Bollingen. Princeton, NJ

Katezenbach, J R and Smith, D K (1994) *Teams at the top.* The Mckinsey Quarterly

Kolb D A and Fry, R (1975) *Toward an applied theory of experiential learning. in C. Cooper (ed.), Theories of Group Process,* London: John Wiley

Maslow, A (1987) *Motivation and personality.* Harper and Row, New York

Menzies Lyth, I (1988) *"Bion's Contribution to Thinking About Groups"* in Grostein, J (ed) *"Do I Dare Disturb the Universe? A memorial to Wilfred R Bion."* Karmac Books, Great Britain

Miller, G A (1956) *The magical number seven, plus or minus two: Some limits on our capacity for processing information. Psychological Review*, 63/2:81-97

Morgan, G (1997) *Images of Organization.* SAGE publications, California

Obholzer, A and Roberts, V Z (eds) (1994) *The unconscious at work.* Routledge, London

Osterman, P (2009) *Recognising the value of Middle Management.* Ivey Business Journal

Peter, L and Hull, R (1969) *The Peter Principle: Why things always go wrong.* William Morrow and Company, New York

Sanderson, B (2010), *The way of kings.* Orion Publishing Group, London

Schein, E H (1992) *Organisational culture and leadership.* Jossey-Bass, San Francisco

Senge, P (1990) *The Fifth Discipline.* London: Century Business

Steward, H; Davies, A and Dick, D (1999) *The Johari Window and the Dark Side of Organisations.* Southern Cross University

Tyson, T (1998) *Working with groups.* Macmillan Education, Australia

Vaughan, D (1996) *The Challenger launch decision.* University of Chicago Press, Chicago

Viggers, J et al (2013) *Melbourne's Water Catchments.* CSIRO Publishing, Melbourne

Wilson, G (1995) *Self-managed teamworking.* Pitman, London

Yunus, M and Jolis, A (2004) *Banker to the Poor: micro-lending and the battle against world poverty.* New York: PublicAffairs, United States

Zimbardo, P (2007) *The Lucifer Effect: Understanding How Good People Turn Evil.* Random House

Index

About the author

Peter has worked as a professional engineer for nearly thirty years, mostly within the water industry. He commenced his career in private industry. He later moved into the public sector and also gained a post graduate diploma in organisational dynamics.

In 2003 Peter founded his own consultancy, PBJ & Associates. Peter and his colleagues have been providing advice on creating value for businesses through the appropriate use of engineering, resource management and organisational structure. PBJ & Associates works with organisations to improve performance through a methodology of developing clear objectives which are outcome focused and process oriented.

As the result of the operation of his own business coupled with his experience working in teams in the private and public sectors, Peter has gained particular insights into the management of organisations, the optimisation of human resources, facilitation of teamwork and the implementation of operational processes to enhance business and professional outcomes.

Peter has also been involved with various non-for-profit and community organisations. Over the years, Peter has found that the principles and processes he has implemented in business are applicable to any organisation seeking to 'create awesome outcomes'.

www.pbj.com.au